Introduction and Acknowledgements

Twenty-seven years ago, in 1972, a list of Grimsby & Immingham tickets was circulated to five prominent members of the Society, Roger Atkinson, the late W.H.Bett, Godfrey Croughton, David Geldard and John Shelbourn. The information given by those members provided the foundation from which this work has developed and also made it clear that the tickets of the line could not be properly understood without a knowledge of the fares structure. Thus, a significant part of the work consists of a detailed study of the fares charged over the years. That production has taken so long is an indication of the complications which have arisen and have resulted in the draft being "put to one side" on occasions. However, now, better late than never, the finished work is offered for your interest. This could not have happened without the help of many people, including the five gentlemen named above and many other Society members who have contributed with details of tickets in their collections. I am deeply indebted to the late John Price (whose book, *The Tramways of Grimsby, Immingham & Cleethorpes*; Light Rail Transit Association, 1991, provides a more detailed background to the line than was possible in this work) for making available his notes of press and other references to the Grimsby & Immingham. The map has been provided by John Gillham to whom our thanks are due and illustrations (tickets, photographs and timetables) have been provided by Godfrey Croughton, Trefor David, David Geldard, John Gillham, Geoffrey Hoyle, Graham Page, the late John Price, Michael Stewart and Glynn Waite. Finally my personal thanks are due to David Harman for taking my draft and adding illustrations to make up the finished work.

Brian Pask
Ilford, Essex
September 1999

Index

1	General Background	3
2	Fares	6
3	Tickets - General	13
4	Great Central Railway Tickets	14
5	Single Tickets - LNER Period	18
6	Workmans Tickets - LNER Period	28
7	Other Ticket Types - LNER Period	31
8	Single, Early Morning Return and Special Cheap Day Tickets - Post 1952	36
9	Other Tickets - Post 1952	44
10	Other Miscellaneous Tickets - Post 1952	50
Appendix	Basis of Railway Fares	53

Great Central.

GRIMSBY AND IMMINGHAM
ELECTRIC RAILWAY.

TIME TABLE OF CARS.
WEEK-DAYS.

GRIMSBY (Corporation Bridge) depart—			IMMINGHAM DOCK depart—		
a.m.	a.m.	p.m.	a.m.	p.m.	p.m.
A 5 15	10 0	c 4 40	B12 20 M.	12 10 S.O.	B 5 10 S.X.
A 5 17	10 40	c 4 50 S.X.	D 5 50	12 20 S.O.	B 5 20
A 5 20	11 20	c 5 20	D 6 0	12 40	B 5 30 S.X.
A 5 25	noon	c 5 40 S.X.	D 6 40	1 0 S.O.	B 6 0
A 5 30	12 0	c 6 0	D 7 20	1 20	B 6 20
A 6 0	p.m.	c 6 40	D 7 40	2 0	B 6 40
A 6 20	12 40	c 7 20	D 8 0	2 40	B 7 20
A 6 40	1 0 S.O.	c 8 0	8 40	3 20	B 8 0
A 7 0	1 20	8 40	9 20	B 4 0	B 8 40
A 7 20	2 0	9 20	10 0	B 4 20	B 9 20
A 8 0	2 40	10 0	10 40	B 4 40	B10 0
A 8 20	3 20	10 40	11 20	B 4 50 S.X.	B10 40
A 8 40	c 4 0	11 20	noon	B 5 0 S.X.	B11 20
9 20			12 0	B 5 5 S.X.	

SUNDAYS.

GRIMSBY (Corporation Bridge) depart—			IMMINGHAM DOCK depart—		
a.m.	p.m.	p.m.	a.m.	p.m.	p.m.
6 0	1 0	6 20	12 20	12 20	5 40
8 0	1 40	7 0	7 0	1 0	6 20
9 0	2 20	7 40	9 0	1 40	7 0
9 40	3 0	8 20	9 40	2 20	7 40
10 20	3 40	9 0	10 20	3 0	8 20
11 0	4 20	9 40	11 0	3 40	9 0
11 40	5 0	10 40	11 40	4 20	9 40
p.m.	5 40	11 50		5 0	10 20
12 20					11 15

S.O. Saturdays only.   S.X. Saturdays excepted.   M. Mondays excepted.

The Cars stop at the following places :—

YARBORO' STREET.   **CLEVELAND BRIDGE.**
STORTFORD STREET.   **IMMINGHAM TOWN.**

and by request at JACKSON STREET, BOULEVARD RECREATION
GROUND, GREAT COATES LEVEL CROSSING, MARSH ROAD
LEVEL CROSSING & KILN LANE LEVEL CROSSING.

FARES.

Grimsby (Corporation Bridge)	and Cleveland Bridge ...	1d.
" "	and Great Coates Level Crossing	2d.
" "	and Marsh Road Level Crossing	4d.
" "	and Kiln Lane Level Crossing	5d.
" "	and Immingham Town	5d.
" "	and Immingham Dock	6d.
Cleveland Bridge	and Great Coates Level Crossing	1d.
"	and Marsh Road Level Crossing	3d.
"	and Kiln Lane Level Crossing	4d.
"	and Immingham Town	4d.
"	and Immingham Dock	5d.
Great Coates Level Crossing	and Marsh Road Level Crossing	2d.
" "	and Kiln Lane Level Crossing	3d.
" "	and Immingham Town	4d.
" "	and Immingham Dock	5d.
Marsh Road Level Crossing	and Kiln Lane Level Crossing	1d.
" "	and Immingham Town	2d.
" "	and Immingham Dock	3d.
Kiln Lane Level Crossing	and Immingham Town	1d.
" "	and Immingham Dock	2d.
Immingham Town	and Immingham Dock	2d.

WORKMEN'S DAILY RETURN TICKETS, Grimsby to Immingham Dock ... ... 3d.
Are issued to bona-fide Workmen by Cars marked "A" available to return by Cars
marked "B," and Workmen's Nightly Return Tickets are issued by Cars marked "C"
available to return by Cars marked "D."
On Saturdays only, Workmen's Daily Return Tickets are available to return by any
Car after 12 noon.

Marylebone Station,
London, N.W., January 15th, 1915.
SSO—14145. (G. N. O.

SAM FAY,
General Manager.

Great Central Railway timetable - 15th January 1915

During the years prior to the First World War, the Great Central Railway wished to expand its dock activities in Lincolnshire. It did so by building a completely new port at Immingham, on the south bank of the Humber some seven miles north west of Grimsby. Prior to this the railways in the area had consisted of the main line into Grimsby from the west with a branch from a triangular junction at Barnetby/Habrough to New Holland (for the ferry to Hull) and a goods only branch from near Great Coates into the western end of the docks at Grimsby. To link the new port with these existing lines three new railways were built:-

(1) The Humber Commercial Railway from Ulceby, on the branch to New Holland.
(2) The Grimsby District Light Railway from Pyewipe Junction, on the dock branch just west of Grimsby.
(3) The Barton and Immingham Light Railway from Goxhill, just south of New Holland.

The first of these was intended primarily as the freight access to the docks, although some passenger services have been provided on all three lines. That which concerns us here is the Grimsby District Light Railway, the main passenger link between Grimsby and the new port. At first this link was provided by a service of steam railmotors between Pyewipe Halt, Grimsby (also referred to as Pyewipe *Road*) and Immingham Halt (sometimes Immingham *Road* Halt), at the eastern end of the dock estate. This service commenced on 3rd January 1910.

As traffic built up and the number of men employed at the dock increased, a more satisfactory link was needed. This was provided by constructing an electric tramway, known as the Grimsby and Immingham Electric Railway, but legally part of the Grimsby District Light Railway. This started at Corporation Bridge, Grimsby and ran for 1½ miles as a street tramway to Cleveland Bridge, where it took up a position on its own right of way alongside the Grimsby District Light Railway nearly to Immingham. Here it left the railway again to terminate by the road into the dock near Immingham village (a location referred to later by the railway as "Immingham Town"). This first section was opened on 15th May 1912, and the rail-motor service on the Grimsby District Light Railway ceased from the same date. Later, extensions were built into Immingham village at Queens Road, and by reversing at Immingham Town, along the road into the docks to a new terminus ("Immingham Dock") just east of the main dock entrance. The Queens Road extension never carried public traffic, but that into the dock estate opened on 17th November 1913.

The stopping places on the line were:-

Grimsby (Corporation Bridge)
Sometimes referred to just as Corporation Bridge.

Yarboro' Street

Jackson Street

Beeson Street
So named on tickets, but timetables referred to "Boulevard Recreation Ground".

Stortford Street

Cleveland Street
Spencer Street until the mid 1930s. There is some doubt about when this became a stopping place. There was a passing loop here at which short workings from

Corporation Bridge (mentioned below) terminated. However it is not in the list of stopping places in the timetable for April 1934, appearing (as Cleveland Street) by April 1935. Tickets with Spencer Street as a stage exist from the early 1930s.

Cleveland Bridge
Usually "Grimsby (Cleveland Bridge)" after 1956. The original stopping place was at the loop well beyond the end of the street tramway section. From 1956 this remained as the alighting point, but cars loaded rather nearer Grimsby.

Great Coates Level Crossing
"Level Crossing" sometimes omitted from tickets.

No.5 Passing Place
Served a rifle range which predated the tramway and may thus have been an unadvertised stopping place from 1912. There is ticket evidence of its use by the First World War. It seems to have become a regular stop by September 1928.

Marsh Road Level Crossing
"Level Crossing" sometimes omitted from tickets. Also, a GCR ticket is known on which it is referred to (probably in error) as "Marsh L Level Crossing".

Kiln Lane Level Crossing
Two GCR tickets are known with the names "Stallingboro' No.8 Loop" and "Kiln Lane No.8", although at this period most tickets showed just "Kiln Lane". LNER tickets showed the name as above, but timetables had "Kiln Lane Level Crossing (Stallingboro')" or "Kiln Lane (Stallingborough)" and the 1959 exchange tickets had the last named version.

Immingham Town
The original 1912 terminus (just "Immingham" on tickets) was east of the road into the docks. With the opening of the extension, cars stopped at the point where they reversed in the centre of this road.

Eastern Entrance to Immingham Dock
Just "Eastern Entrance" on the one ticket to show it. A request stop here was in use for a time during and after the First World War, perhaps in connection with wartime security arrangements at the docks. Not in Bradshaw for July 1916, it is in timetables for July 1917 (Bradshaw), May 1919 (GCR) and July 1920 (Bradshaw), but not August 1921.

Immingham Dock

As can be seen, there was some inconsistency over names at times, and in two cases timetables and tickets normally used different names. All are shown in timetables as request stops only except for the termini and Yarboro' Street, Stortford Street, Cleveland Bridge and Immingham Town. However, it is understood that Cleveland Bridge was, in practice, not observed as a compulsory stop and this may also have applied to the others. In no sense could any be termed 'stations', although there was an office and waiting shelter at Corporation Bridge and, in the final years, a small office at Cleveland Bridge. A waiting shelter was also provided at Immingham Dock and later at Kiln Lane as well.

The services provided over the Grimsby and Immingham Electric Railway did not vary much throughout its existence, with a roughly half-hourly frequency throughout the day, an all night service and an intensive peak period service. Timetables of 1915, 1919, 1945, 1952, 1956 and 1959 are shown on pages 2, 17, 25, 43, 52 and 49. For a short time a

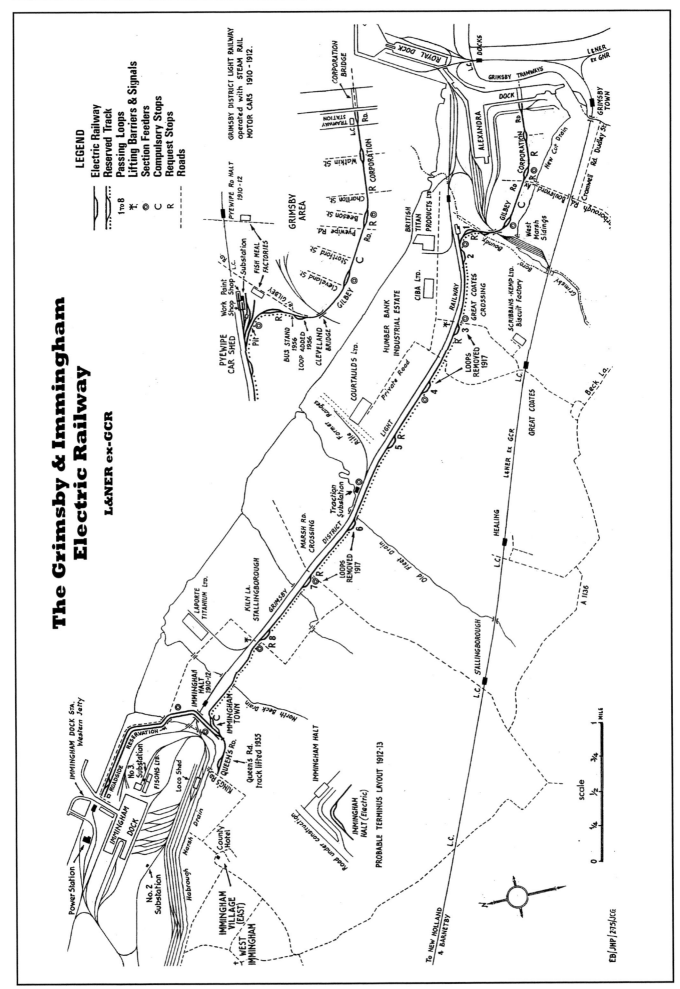

The Grimsby & Immingham Electric Railway

L&NER ex-GCR

LEGEND

══	Electric Railway
	Reserved Track
	Passing Loops
1 to 8	
*	Lifting Barriers & Signals
◎	Section Feeders
C	Compulsory Stops
R	Request Stops
---	Roads

local service operated over part of the street tramway section between Corporation Bridge and Spencer Street (later Cleveland Street). This is said to have commenced from 10th September 1928 and ceased in 1930 (both 15th January and 11th February being quoted for its withdrawal) following competition from the parallel *Grimsby Corporation* bus service (introduced 15th December 1929). However, it did not disappear from timetables until some time later, appearing in the LNER timetable for May 1932 and Bradshaw for April 1933, but not in the LNER timetable for May 1933 or Bradshaw for July 1933. Even allowing for the fact that timetables could be slightly late in reflecting a change such as this, all that can be said with certainty is that the service had ceased by mid-1933. This is confirmed by the late W.H. Bett, who visited the line on 31st July 1933 and found that the service had ceased by then. It is perhaps possible that the regular service ceased in 1930, leaving some residual service which continued to 1933. Later, from 1st July 1956, the street tramway section was closed and replaced by a local bus service which connected with the trams at Cleveland Bridge.

For many years the tramway remained the only link between Grimsby and Immingham, apart from a limited workman's service on the Humber Commercial Railway via Ulceby. The absence of a competing bus service is explained by the lack of a reasonably direct road route and the relatively small resident population in the Immingham area (many of whom would have been railwaymen and their families and thus less likely to use any alternative bus service). Never really profitable, the tramway had always been regarded as essential to, and therefore a charge on, the dock undertaking. However by the late 1950s, the finances of the tramway were considered in isolation and attempts were made to find a replacement. That eventually decided upon was a bus service operated jointly by *Grimsby Corporation* and *Lincolnshire Road Car Co.* (route 45) between Grimsby and Immingham Dock which commenced operation from 28th September 1959. Of necessity this had to use the indirect road route and, probably for this reason, its effectiveness as a peak period carrier was in some doubt. Thus, initially, the tramway was retained with a peak period service, but all off-peak and night traffic ceased with the introduction of the bus service. During this period there was co-ordination of fares and some interavailability of tickets between the tramway, the bus and the workman's train via Ulceby. After these arrangements had been in operation for some time, it was found that (probably because of the growth of private transport) the buses could cope adequately with the peak period traffic, and from 3rd July 1961 the tramway closed completely.

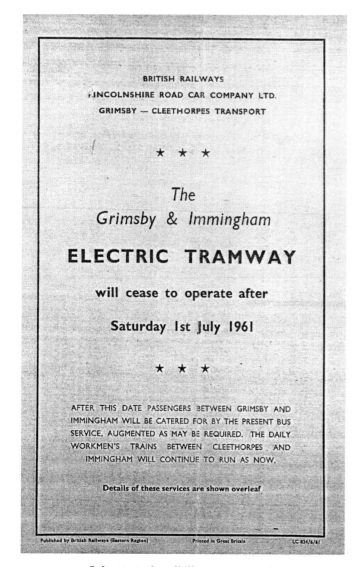

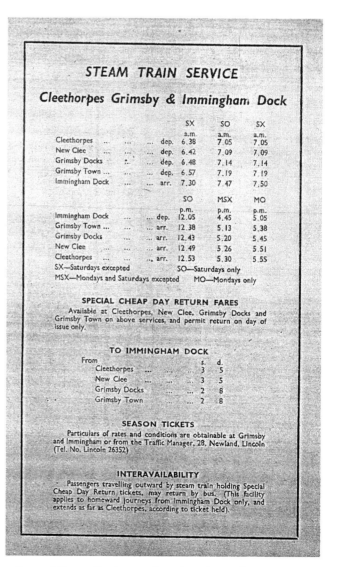

July 1961 - handbill announcing closure and showing times of the continuing workmen's train service between Immingham and Cleethorpes. The timetable for replacement bus route 45 was shown inside.

2 - Fares (see also Appendix A)

The Grimsby District Light Railway Order 1906, Section 41, specified that fares to be charged were to be "as on the Company's railway undertaking". The throughout single fare (to Immingham Town only at that stage) on opening on 15th May 1912 was 5d and the *Grimsby Telegraph* for 15th November 1913, covering the opening of the extension to Immingham Dock, gave a single fare of 6d. For journeys of 5 miles 34 chains and 6 miles 57 chains these were just below the 1d per mile which was normal (but not invariable) railway practice for third class single fares at this time. Handbills dated January and November 1915 have been seen which include a fare scale with single fares as shown below. No fares are shown for No.5 Passing Place (probably in use, but unadvertised at this stage) or Eastern Entrance (not opened until later), but these have been added on the basis of ticket evidence. The two fares in brackets have not been confirmed, but seem likely in comparison with the remainder. The only evidence of a fare to Eastern Entrance is that shown, and it seems probable that the Immingham Dock fare applied for all other bookings.

Corporation Bridge								
1d	Cleveland Bridge							
2d	1d	Great Coates Level Crossing						
(3d)	2d	1d	No.5 Passing Place					
4d	3d	2d	1d	Marsh Road Level Crossing				
5d	4d	3d	2d	1d	Kiln Lane Level Crossing			
5d	4d	4d	(3d)	2d	1d	Immingham Town		
							Eastern Entrance	
6d	5d	5d	4d	3d	2d	2d	1d	Immingham Dock

The few early tickets seen are in accordance with this scale and the evidence suggests that it applied from the opening of the line up to the First World War period. Evidence of fares other than singles is sadly lacking, and all that can be said is that the workman's return fare was 3d for the throughout journey in 1913 and 1915 (again probably applying from the opening up to the First World War) and there was a privilege return fare of 3d between Corporation Bridge and Immingham Town.

If normal railway practice had been followed, the single fares would have been increased from 1st January 1917 by 50% and from 6th August 1920 (1st September for workmen's fares) to 75% over the pre-1917 levels. From 1st January 1923 railway fares generally were reduced to 50% over their pre-1917 levels and a major revision took place from 1st January 1928, with single fares re-calculated at 1½d per mile. This should have given throughout single fares of 9d (1917), 10½d (1920), 9d (1923) and 10½d (1928). This is where problems arise, however, as ticket evidence indicates throughout single fares of 8d followed by 10½d, the latter fare also applying after the 1928 revision. Workman's fares were not generally increased with the 1917 revision, but a new mileage scale (often involving a considerable increase) was introduced in 1920 and some reductions followed in 1928.

To clarify the position, we have to resort to the selective and rather less reliable evidence of contemporary press reports. The *Grimsby News* for 19th January 1917 reported "Since the appearance of last week's *News*, the Great Central Railway have dropped the increased fares which were charged from the beginning of the year. Great hardship was felt by many who continually travel on the cars and doubtless strong representations from an influential quarter have been made to induce the company to forego the fifty per cent increase". However, the fragmentary fare scale below, reconstructed from ticket evidence, confirms that there were increases:-

Corporation Bridge								
-	Cleveland Bridge							
3d	-	Great Coates Level Crossing						
-	3d	-	No.5 Passing Place					
-	-	3d	-	Marsh Road Level Crossing				
-	-	-	3d	-	Kiln Lane Level Crossing			
6d	-	-	-	3d	-	Immingham Town		
-	-	-	-	-	-	-	Eastern Entrance	
8d	-	-	6d	-	-	-	-	Immingham Dock

This seems to suggest a 50% increase with one or two politically sensitive fares such as Grimsby to Immingham Town and Dock reduced somewhat! It is clear that the GCR intended to apply the standard increase but was either persuaded not to or reduced fares again after increasing them. The date of the press report suggests the former. It seems unlikely that the company would have been persuaded within 19 days to change its mind and reverse an already implemented increase. It is far more likely that protests following advance information of the increase (which would have been readily available in a railway community such as Immingham) resulted in it being modified prior to introduction.

The next evidence of fares is provided by a report in the *Grimsby News* for 5th September 1919 on a strike by railway staff at Immingham which began the previous Friday (i.e. 29th August 1919). This strike had its origins in a change in the travel arrangements for locomen at Immingham who lived in Grimsby. Up to 1917 these men were paid travelling time and given free passes for the tram. The press report explains the post-1917 position thus *"The railwaymen receive 11/- per day, pay their own fare and come on pay when they reach Immingham. At the end of the week, half the car fares are refunded, making the men's nett wages 10/10 per day."*. What actually provoked the 1919 strike was introduction of similar arrangements for boilermakers at Immingham. It is not clear where these men worked and thus whether they travelled to Immingham Town (as the locomen would) or Immingham Dock. It is clear that the daily fare for the men referred to in the press report was then 4d, but whether this represented the fare to Immingham Town or Immingham Dock is not clear. There is no other evidence of a workman's return fare of 4d, and we are thus left with the thought that this might be the privilege return fare. However, railwaymen on or travelling to duty would be unlikely to pay privilege fares, which in their conditions of issue have always specifically precluded use for duty and residential journeys. If, exceptionally, they did here, privilege fares have always been based on half single fare for return journey - i.e. with a 50% increase over prewar fares, 4d to Immingham Town and 4½d to Immingham Dock. On the basis of the single fares of 6d and 8d shown above these would be 3d and 4d. The strike was eventually settled and work resumed on 19th September on the basis of payment of 1/- per day travelling time and a full refund of car fares.

Despite the suggestion above of a workman's return fare of 4d in 1917, the only evidence seen for these fares is in the timetables, which show the fare from Grimsby to Immingham Dock. This was still 3d in the timetable for May 1919, becoming 8d by October 1921.

Ticket evidence is that the 1920 increase was applied - the throughout fare certainly reached its full 75% increase level of 10½d. It is therefore reasonable to use this basis to reconstruct a fare scale for singles at this period. Those fares which are confirmed by tickets seen are indicated by an asterisk.

Corporation Bridge							
2d	Cleveland Bridge						
3½d*	2d	Great Coates Level Crossing					
5½d	(3½d)	2d	No.5 Passing Place				
7d	5½d	3½d*	2d	Marsh Road Level Crossing			
9d*	7d	5½d	3½d*	2d	Kiln Lane Level Crossing		
9d*	7d	7d	5½d	3½d*	2d	Immingham Town	
10½d*	9d*	9d*	7d	5½d	(3½d)	3½d*	Immingham Dock

The 3½d ticket seen does not include the bookings Cleveland Bridge / No.5 Passing Place and Kiln Lane / Immingham Dock (in brackets above), suggesting that the fares for these journeys were exceptional in not taking the standard increase. The 1920 scale for workman's return fares gives, for the 6 miles 57 chains from Corporation Bridge to Immingham Dock, a fare of 9d. However, this conflicts with the only evidence of workman's fares at this period, the reference in timetables to the fare for that journey. This is shown as 8d in all timetables between October 1921 and July 1926 which have been checked, suggesting an increase from 3d to 8d from 1st September 1920. Why the permitted increase to 9d was not applied is unclear - certainly even this high level would have just been within the permitted increase limit!

The local authority with Immingham's interests at heart, Grimsby Rural District Council, claimed credit for persuading the LNER, from 1st September 1923, to:-
a) reintroduce the 1/- cheap day return Immingham Town or Dock to Grimsby
b) give child fares to children of 3 but under 12 years
c) make workman's returns and seasons available to as well as from Grimsby

The report of these changes suggests that the throughout single fare after 1st September was 10½d, but not whether it changed from that date. Also the reference to the cheap day return was specifically to its *re*introduction from Immingham to Grimsby. There clearly had previously been a cheap fare of some sort, but the inference could be either that a facility already available in one direction only (from Grimsby) became available in both directions or that a facility previously withdrawn completely had been reintroduced.

The whole tenor of the above report is that the 1923 fare reduction was not applied to the Grimsby & Immingham, hence the complaints! It is therefore surprising that there is ticket evidence (albeit of unissued tickets) for lower fares, in accordance with the scale below, at about this time.

Corporation Bridge							
2d	Cleveland Bridge						
-	2d	Great Coates Level Crossing					
4d	-	2d	No.5 Passing Place				
5d	4d	-	2d	Marsh Road Level Crossing			
-	-	4d	-	2d	Kiln Lane Level Crossing		
-	5d	-	4d	-	2d	Immingham Town	
-	7d	-	-	5d	4d	2d	Immingham Dock

The 4d ticket actually shows a stage from Marsh Road to Immingham Dock (a stage also shown on the 5d), but this is altered in manuscript to Kiln Lane. It seems probable that the version shown in the table above is correct. The 2d fare Immingham Town to Dock is also suspect (although not amended) and may have arisen from the old 1d Eastern Entrance to Immingham Dock stage being incorrectly carried forward from an earlier ticket. It is clear that the fare scale represented by these tickets was not to a straight 50% over 1917 levels, some fares being above this level, some below it (perhaps in order to avoid odd ½d fares).

In 1925, the Parish Council complained that the Grimsby & Immingham workman's fares were the highest in the country and asked that cheap day returns to Grimsby should be issued all day. The 3½d fare (presumably, but not necessarily, workman's) from Immingham Town to Dock was specifically mentioned as too high and is said to have been reduced subsequently to 3d. It is difficult to comment on this, since we do not know what the Immingham Town to Dock workman's fare was earlier. (Surprisingly, there is no ticket evidence of a workman's fare for this journey at any time.) However, it is clear that the single fare for this journey (of 1 mile 23 chains) was always well over standard - 2d in 1915, when 1d or at most 1½d would have been expected; perhaps 3d in 1917, 3½d in 1920 and 3d in 1928, when the distance would have indicated 2½d. Thus the reduction may have been to the single fare, which was 3½d in 1920 and 3d by 1928.

In a later press report (of 3rd August 1928) the LNER announced that cheap return tickets at 1/- would be issued every day from Grimsby to Immingham (Dock or Town), available outward by any car after 9am, return by any car same day. It is not clear whether this was merely an advertisement of what was available at that time or an announcement of some improvement which was about to (or had just) taken place. However, the latter is possible since there is ticket evidence of more restricted availability for these tickets in early LNER days.

It is possible to reconstruct from ticket evidence a post 1928 single fare scale for the main part of the line. This is shown below with (in brackets) the standard 1928 fare for the distance concerned where this differed:-

Corporation Bridge/Stortford Street							
2½d *	Cleveland Bridge						
3d	2½d(1½d)	Great Coates Level Crossing					
5½d(4½d)	3d	2½d	No 5 Passing Place				
7d	5½d(4½d)	3½d(4d)	2½d	Marsh Road Level Crossing			
9d(7½d)	7½d(5½d)	5½d(4½d)	3d	2½d(1½d)	Kiln Lane Level Crossing		
9d(8½d)	7½d(7d)	7d(6d)	5½d(4d)	3d(2½d)	2½d(1½d)	Immingham Town	
10½d	9d(8½d)	9d(7½d)	7d(6d)	6d(4½d)	4½d(4d)	3d(2½d)	Immingham Dock

* Later reduced to 2d - see below

It will be seen that, although the throughout fare and a few others were standard, most of the intermediate fares were above standard and only one below (Great Coates and Marsh Road, highlighted above). The post 1928 workman's return fare for the throughout journey is confirmed by both timetables and tickets as 7½d. The earliest timetable seen with this fare is that for July 1929, while that for July 1926 still shows 8d. This is consistent with a reduction from 8d (the presumed 1920 fare) to 7½d from 1st January 1928.

It is impossible to be dogmatic on the basis of the information available. To summarise, however, the following seems to have been the likely effect of the various fare changes:-

1917 full increase on single fares originally intended, but modified in some respects after protests. Workman's fares not increased.

1920 clearly applied to both single and workman's fares (but the latter not quite to the full permitted level).

1923 evidence conflicting, but if the ticket evidence for a fare reduction is accepted, it was not to a straight 50% over 1917.

1928 if fares were reduced in 1923, they were clearly increased again later (presumably from 1928). However, 1928 single fares are very similar to those which would have resulted from a full 75% increase in 1920 and it is tempting to suggest that (with a few local exceptions) these fares survived 1923 and 1928 unchanged. Workman's fare was reduced from 1920 level.

One interesting feature is the lack of recorded protests over the massive increase in the workman's fare in 1920. However, the workers involved in the 1919 strike had their fares paid for them by this time, and this may well have taken much of the heat out of the issue.

Whether the scale quoted above originated with the 1928 revision or not, it was used as the base for subsequent revisions as if it had. Thus for the next 24 years Grimsby and Immingham fares were calculated by applying the appropriate standard railway percentage fare increases to this base. This also applied for workman's fares, which will be dealt with in greater detail later. The actual single fares were:-

From 1st October 1937 ("N" fares)

Corporation Bridge/Stortford Street							
2½d	Cleveland Bridge						
3½d	2½d	Great Coates Level Crossing					
6d	3½d	2½d	No 5 Passing Place				
7½d	6d	4d	2½d	Marsh Road Level Crossing			
9½d	8d	6d	3½d	2½d	Kiln Lane Level Crossing		
9½d	8d	7½d	6d	3½d	2½d	Immingham Town	
11d	9½d	9½d	7½d	6½d	5d	3½d	Immingham Dock

From 1st May 1940 ("R" fares)

Corporation Bridge/Stortford Street							
2½d	Cleveland Bridge						
3½d	2½d	Great Coates Level Crossing					
7d	3½d	2½d	No 5 Passing Place				
8½d	7d	4d	2½d	Marsh Road Level Crossing			
10½d	9d	7d	3½d	2½d	Kiln Lane Level Crossing		
10½d	9d	8½d	7d	3½d	2½d	Immingham Town	
1/-	10½d	10½d	8½d	7½d	6d	3½d	Immingham Dock

From 1st December 1940 ("C" fares)

Corporation Bridge/Stortford Street							
2½d	*Cleveland Bridge*						
4½d	2½d	*Great Coates Level Crossing*					
7d	4½d	2½d	*No 5 Passing Place*				
8½d	7d	5d	2½d	*Marsh Road Level Crossing*			
11½d	9d	7d	4½d	2½d	*Kiln Lane Level Crossing*		
11½d	9d	8½d	7d	4½d	2½d	*Immingham Town*	
1/1	11½d	11½d	8½d	7½d	6d	4½d	*Immingham Dock*

From 1st July 1946 ("P" fares)

Corporation Bridge/Stortford Street							
3½d	*Cleveland Bridge*						
4½d	3½d	*Great Coates Level Crossing*					
8d	4½d	3½d	*No 5 Passing Place*				
10½d	8d	5d	3½d	*Marsh Road Level Crossing*			
1/0½d	11d	8d	4½d	3½d	*Kiln Lane Level Crossing*		
1/0½d	11d	10½d	8d	4½d	3½d	*Immingham Town*	
1/3	1/0½d	1/0½d	10½d	8½d	7d	4½d	*Immingham Dock*

From 1st October 1947 ("Z" fares)

Corporation Bridge/Stortford Street							
3½d	*Cleveland Bridge*						
5½d	3½d	*Great Coates Level Crossing*					
9d	5½d	3½d	*No 5 Passing Place*				
11½d	9d	6d	3½d	*Marsh Road Level Crossing*			
1/2½d	1/-	9d	5½d	3½d	*Kiln Lane Level Crossing*		
1/2½d	1/-	11½d	9d	5½d	3½d	*Immingham Town*	
1/5	1/2½d	1/2½d	11½d	10½d	8d	5½d	*Immingham Dock*

The situation on the Corporation Bridge/Cleveland Bridge section is a little more confused, particularly in the period up to 1937. A number of tickets for short journeys on this section are known to exist, and fortunately some of them can be dated with reasonable certainly. The significant stages are:-

2½d	*Corporation Bridge/Cleveland Bridge* *late 1920s*
1½d	*Corporation Bridge/Stortford Street* *late 1920s*
1d	*Corporation Bridge/Beeson Street* *31 Jul 1933*
2d	*Corporation Bridge/Cleveland Bridge* *31 Jul 1933*
1d	*Corporation Bridge/Cleveland Street* *Jul 1937*

The evidence of these and other tickets can only be explained by changes in the fare stages as well as reductions in fares. The latter is not unlikely when it is borne in mind that Grimsby Corporation introduced a bus service parallel to the line as far as Gilbey Road from 15th December 1929.

On the available evidence, the fare scale below is postulated as applying up to the late 1920s:-

Corporation Bridge		
1½d	*Stortford Street*	
2½d	1½d	*Cleveland Bridge*

By 1933 (but probably at about the time the *Grimsby Corporation* bus to Gilbey Road was introduced in 1929), the Corporation Bridge/Cleveland Bridge fare was reduced to 2d and intermediate 1d and 1½d fare stages introduced. Ticket evidence confirms the following fare scale:-

Corporation Bridge			
1d	*Beeson Street*		
1½d	1d	*Spencer Street*	
2d	1½d	1½d	*Cleveland Bridge*

These reductions were evidently not sufficient, and by 1937 the 1d fare from Corporation Bridge extended to Cleveland Street (as Spencer Street had by then become), thus covering virtually the whole of the residential area through which the line passed. There is no evidence of any change in the 2d or 1½d fares to Cleveland Bridge and there is no reason to assume that they were altered at this time. This gave the following fare scale:-

Corporation Bridge			
	Beeson Street		
1d		*Cleveland Street*	
2d	1½d	1½d	*Cleveland Bridge*

In subsequent revisions the above fare scale seems to have been used as a base and the standard scale increases applied, with one minor exception thus:-

From 1st October 1937 ("N" fares)

Corporation Bridge			
	Beeson Street		
1½d		*Cleveland Street*	
2½d	2d	2d	*Cleveland Bridge*

(no change 1st May 1940 or 1st December 1940 - "R" and "C" fares)

From 1st July 1946 ("P" fares)

Corporation Bridge			
	Beeson Street		
2d		*Cleveland Street*	
3½d	2½d	2½d	*Cleveland Bridge*

From 1st October 1947 ("Z" fares)

Corporation Bridge			
	Beeson Street		
2½d		*Cleveland Street*	
3½d	3d	3d	*Cleveland Bridge*

These fares have been confirmed from tickets or handbills. The Beeson Street and Cleveland Street/Cleveland Bridge fare for the "Z" scale is confirmed by a 1951 leaflet as 3d, and ticket evidence indicates the existence also of a 2½d fare for these bookings. This must have been the "P" fare, although the correct scale fare at this time should also have been 3d.

There were, as has been detailed above, workman's fares from the earliest days. Early evidence is of one workman's fare only, from Grimsby to Immingham Dock, at the extremely low rate of 3d return. This, as we have seen, later became 8d (probably in 1920) and 7½d (probably in 1928). Early press reports indicate fairly restricted availability of these tickets to suit working hours at the docks, but this conflicts with information given in timetables, which show much wider availability. The timetable for October 1914 shows workman's tickets as being issued by cars leaving Grimsby between 5.15am and 8.40am (surprisingly late for the issue of workman's tickets at this period) and valid for return by cars leaving Immingham Dock between 4pm and 12.20am, on Saturdays by any car after 12noon. Subsequent changes (and the timetables in which they have been noted) were:-

Outward cars from Grimsby:-

5.15am to 8.40am	Oct 1914, Jan, Jul 1915
3.00am to 8.40am	Nov 1915
3.00am to 9.00am	May 1919, Oct 1921
1.50am to 7.20am	Sep 1924, Jul 1926, Jul 1929, May 1932, May, Jul 1933
12.50am to 7.20am	Apr 1934

Return cars from Immingham Dock:-

4.00pm to 12.20am	Oct 1914, Jan, Jul, Nov 1915,
4.00pm to 12.25am	May 1919
3.55pm to 11.20pm	Oct 1921
4.00pm to 11.20pm	Sep 1924, Jul 1926
4.20pm to 11.20pm	Jul 1929, May 1932, May, Jul 1933, Apr 1934

Return cars on Saturdays:-

after 12 noon	Oct 1914, Jan, Jul, Nov 1915
after 11.15am	May 1919, Oct 1921
after 11.00am	Sep 1924, Jul 1926, Jul 1929, May 1932, May, Jul 1933, Apr 1934

Identical information to that in the April 1934 timetable appeared in subsequent LNER/BR timetables and Bradshaws up to September 1951 (the last issue prior to the abolition of workman's returns in 1952).

In addition to the above, timetables from 1914 to 1919 show workman's nightly tickets (at the same fare as the daily workman's) available outward from Grimsby between 4pm and 8pm and to return from Immingham Dock between 6am (5.50am by January 1915, 3.47am by November 1915) and 8am (8.25am by May 1919). This facility is not shown in the October 1921 timetable or later and was presumably withdrawn. However, normal railway practice was to issue (on an unadvertised basis) night workman's tickets wherever there was a daily fare on production by the workman concerned of a form of identity confirming that he was a bona fide night worker. LNER workman's tickets have punch spaces for "day" and "night", suggesting that by this time the generally available and advertised facility had been replaced by an unadvertised one available only to those holding the appropriate form of identity. There is ticket evidence of the existence in 1945 of six and seven day workman's tickets for the Corporation Bridge/Immingham Dock journey at six or seven times the daily fare. Whether this was a wartime facility only or existed earlier is not known.

The absence of workman's fares on the street tramway section is recorded as causing intermittent complaints and the representations in 1923 by the District Council suggest that originally workman's returns were available only from Grimsby to Immingham, but that, from 1st September 1923,

they were introduced in the opposite direction also. By early LNER days a rather wider range of workman's fares (including one between Corporation Bridge and Cleveland Bridge) were available, and these seem to have been more or less arbitrarily fixed at rather less than the single fare. Some bookings were available in either direction, but others seem to have been given in one direction only.

So far only single and workman's return fares have been mentioned. The 1923 report mentioned above implies that child fares had not previously been available but were introduced from 1st September 1923. Certainly they continued on the normal half fare basis (both for singles and the other types of ticket to be mentioned) right through LNER days. There was also a wide range of other railway type facilities available, many of them from the earliest days, and these will now be discussed in more detail.

The 1923 report also implies that a 1/- cheap day return between Immingham and Grimsby had been available prior to this date but, as we have already said, exactly what happened from 1st September 1923 is unclear. A cheap fare obviously had existed previously, but whether it then became available in both directions or was reintroduced after having been withdrawn completely is in doubt. A cheap fare which is known to have existed in 1923 (an LNER ticket with a pencil date of 9/7/1923 has been seen) is a "Pleasure Party One Day Return" to Immingham Town. It is tempting to suggest that this was the predecessor of the cheap day return, but this seems unlikely since the term "pleasure party" was normally applied specifically to tickets for parties and the GCR did have day returns with other titles. It has been suggested elsewhere that this ticket was used for trips to see the liners at Immingham Dock. It may indeed have been used by parties travelling with this objective, or even by parties of passengers from the cruise ships (which were calling at Immingham at this time) having day trips to the delights of Grimsby, (or, more likely, Cleethorpes) but the present writer has seen no evidence for either use and it seems surprising that it is to Immingham *Town* if these uses were contemplated. It would presumably have been available for any party fulfilling the requirements (e.g. party size, time of travel, etc.) of the normal railway "Pleasure Party" facility.

A normal cheap day fare was available in either direction quite early in LNER days and took the appropriate scale increases in 1937 and 1940. It would have been withdrawn with other railway cheap fares in 1942, but is known to have been reintroduced after the war as tickets with the corresponding 1947 fare of 1/8 are known. Ticket evidence shows that the validity of this facility changed twice. In early LNER days the validity was outward between 10am and 4pm, return same day between 10am and 4pm or after 7pm. As we have recorded earlier, by (or perhaps from) 1928 the availability was outward after 9am, return by any car on day of issue and by 1936 had become outward after 7.45am, return by any car on day of issue.

During the war the cheap day fare was (as was normal elsewhere) replaced by a monthly return booking at single fare and a third (although the ticket did not state its validity and gave no indication that it was not an ordinary return). This continued (with appropriate scale increases in 1946 and 1947) until replaced by an ordinary return in 1952. Monthly return fares generally were the subject of an additional fare increase of 10% ("E" fare scale) in 1952. However, a leaflet dated July 1952 confirms that the Grimsby to Immingham fare remained at its "Z" fare level of 1/11, although it had by this time (presumably from 1st May 1952) acquired three month validity.

There is ticket evidence of a privilege return fare in GCR

days between Corporation Bridge and Immingham Town at 3d (the minimum fare for this facility, and thus covering both pre- and post-1917 fares) and 4½d (1920 fare). That such facilities were available from the beginning is indicated by a ticket showing the pre-1913 name "Immingham". There were also in GCR days "naval and military" tickets (both charged, probably at single fare for return journey, and issued on warrant), and dog, folding mail cart and bicycle tickets (at the standard minimum railway rates for these articles). By the Second World War, facilities available for the throughout journey were Service Military, Army and Navy on Leave (later Forces Leave), Privilege (adult and child), Dog, Pram and Bicycle. The rates for these were based on the single fare or distance in accordance with normal railway practice.

There were also special free tickets for the large number of railwaymen travelling on the line on duty. If the reports on the 1919 strike are correct, these will have existed up to 1917

and again from 1919. The tickets appear to have been issued to the men at their depots and given up on the car. A report has also been seen of ordinary tickets stamped with the names of firms, for use as prepaids by the staff of those firms, but no such tickets have been seen by the present writer. Season tickets are known to have existed from their mention in the 1923 report of the District Council representations, and weekly season ticket rates of 2/- (1945), 2/10 (1951/2) and 4/- (1952/3) for the street tramway section are shown in timetable leaflets. There is also evidence of through bookings to both Immingham and Killingholme via Grimsby and the Tramway. Finally, several special tickets exist for trips on the line by the Light Railway Transport League.

The various fares (other than single) which are known to have existed are summarised below, with fares which should have existed, but have not been confirmed, shown in brackets:-

	pre-1937	from 1 Oct 1937	from 1 May 1940	from 1 Dec 1940	from 1 Jul 1946	from 1 Oct 1947
Workman's Fares -						
Corporation Bridge / Cleveland Bridge	2d	2d	2d	2d	(2½d)	3d
Corporation Bridge to Great Coates				*		4½d
Corporation Bridge / Immingham Town	6½d	6½d	7d	7d	(8d)	10d
Corporation Bridge / Immingham Dock	7½d	7½d	8½d	8½d	9½d	11½d
Cleveland Bridge / Immingham Town	6½d			*		
Immingham Town to Great Coates	4½d	4½d	5d	5d	(5½d)	7d
Immingham Dock to Great Coates	6d	6d	6½d	6½d	(7½d)	9½d

(These fares were not all available in both directions. Fares to Great Coates were available only in the direction shown; the position of Cleveland Bridge/Immingham Town is uncertain; the remainder were available in both directions. Those marked* do not appear in January 1945 timetable leaflet.)

Cheap Return -						
Corporation Bridge / Immingham Tn or Dk	1/1	1/1	(1/2)	1/3	(1/5)	1/8

(Facility withdrawn from 1942, during currency of 1/3 fare. It is not known whether reintroduction after the war was prior to July 1946 fare increase (at 1/5) or after this (at 1/8).)

Monthly Return -						
Corporation Bridge / Immingham Dock				1/6	1/8	1/11

(Facility introduced 1942 to replace cheap return, but continued after the latter was reintroduced. Scale increase from 1st January 1952 to 2/1 did *not* apply. Validity altered to 3 months from 1st May 1952.)

The 1952 Charges Scheme put Grimsby & Immingham fares strictly on mileage, rounded to the next whole mile as shown below:-

Corporation Bridge									
1	Beeson Street								
1	1	Cleveland Street							
2	1	1	Cleveland Bridge						
2	2	2	1	Great Coates Level Crossing					
3	3	3	2	2	No 5 Passing Place				
5	4	4	3	3	2	Marsh Road Level Crossing			
5	5	4	4	3	2	1	Kiln Lane Level Crossing		
6	5	5	5	4	3	2	1	Immingham Town	
7	7	6	6	5	4	3	3	2	Immingham Dock

The following rates were applied to this scale:-

Mileage		Fare Scale Letter	1	2	3	4	5	6	7
From 1952	single	H	2d	4d	6d	7d	9d	11d	1/1
	EMR	H	-	6d	8d	9d	11d	1/-	1/2
From 16 Aug 1953	EMR	J	-	6d	8d	10d	1/-	1/2	1/4
(singles not changed)									
From 5 Jun 1955	single	-	2d	4d	6d	8d	10d	1/-	1/2
	EMR	-	-	6d	9d	1/-	1/2	1/4	1/6
From 15 Sep 1957	EMR	-	-	7d	10d	1/1	1/4	1/6	
(singles not changed)									

Despite this apparent simplicity, there were some exceptions in the early days of the Charges Scheme. These arose mostly from the staged implementation of the scheme, by which those fares which were reduced came into operation from 1st May 1952, while those which were increased were not introduced until 1st September. A leaflet dated 1st July 1952 confirms:-

(1) The new single fares had (with two exceptions) been introduced. The two exceptions were Great Coates/No.5 Passing Place and No.5 Passing Place/Marsh Road, which remained at 3½d rather than being increased to 4d. Surprisingly the Corporation Bridge / Cleveland Bridge fare (also 3½d) was increased to 4d.

(2) The existing workman's returns remained in use.

(3) The monthly return fare remained at its previous level although it was now described as a "return" and had three months validity (this was in accordance with normal practice elsewhere).

The leaflet included a footnote "The whole of the above fares are subject to alteration on and from 1st September 1952" and a further leaflet (see page 43) details the changes from this date. The two non-standard single fares were increased, the workman's returns were replaced by early morning returns and the monthly return by an ordinary return at twice the new single fare. However, even then there was one non-standard fare - a 4d EMR replacing the 3d Corporation Bridge/Cleveland Bridge workman's fare (the scale EMR fare of 6d for this booking would have exceeded considerably the 20% increase limit imposed by the Charges Scheme). This non-standard fare is still shown in a leaflet dated June 1953 but would doubtless have been eliminated at the 1953 or 1955 revision.

It will be seen that, because of the short distance between stops, fares existed (and hence tickets were required) for each mileage graduation from 1 mile up to 7 miles. Later, with the cut back of the line to Cleveland Bridge from 1st July 1956 only fares up to 6 miles existed. During the interim period in 1952, old tickets will have remained in use for those fares which did not change.

For the last few years of the existence of the line, following the restriction of the service to peak periods only, completely new fares were introduced. These were higher than standard BR fares and were related to (but not the same as) the fares charged on the parallel bus service. Because of the non-standard nature of the fares, the early morning returns were replaced by special cheap days. The new fare scales, which came into operation from 28th September 1959 and lasted until the closure of the line, are shown below:-

Singles

Cleveland Bridge						
3d	Great Coates Level Crossing					
5d	5d	No 5 Passing Place				
8d	8d	5d	Marsh Road Level Crossing			
11d	8d	5d	3d	Kiln Lane Level Crossing		
1/1	10d	8d	5d	3d	Immingham Town	
1/3	1/1	10d	8d	8d	5d	Immingham Dock

Special Cheap Day Returns

Cleveland Bridge						
-	Great Coates Level Crossing					
-	-	No 5 Passing Place				
1/2	1/2	-	Marsh Road Level Crossing			
1/8	1/2	-	-	Kiln Lane Level Crossing		
2/1	1/6	1/2	-	-	Immingham Town	
2/1	1/10	1/6	1/2	1/2	-	Immingham Dock

After 1952 the various additional fares for the throughout journey continued, with ordinary returns, privilege returns and forces leave singles and returns based on the revised single fares. With the cut-back of the line in 1956 these were, of course, modified to apply from Cleveland Bridge instead of Corporation Bridge and the fares reduced accordingly. Since it was simply twice the single fare, the ordinary return seems to have gradually died out. There is no evidence of an ordinary return after 1956 and in any case there would be virtually no demand for one after the introduction of the special cheap days in 1959. The reduced fares, however, continued until the final closure of the line. The through fares to Immingham and Killingholme survived closure of the street tramway section (see page 43), (although not available on the bus between Corporation Bridge and Cleveland Bridge), but were withdrawn from 28th September 1959.

3 - Tickets - General

As with fares, Grimsby and Immingham tickets represent a mixture of railway and tramway practice. Even though 'stations' existed at the two termini and (at least in the final years) at Cleveland Bridge, all local tickets were punch type and issued on the cars by conductors. However, the line was also regarded as part of the railway network in that through bookings (with normal railway type tickets) were available from various stations to Immingham and Killingholme via Grimsby and the tramway. The punch type tickets issued on the cars can be divided into two groups, the singles (and in later years the early morning returns/special cheap days), and the various other types.

The singles followed tramway practice in that there was one ticket for each fare value covering all the bookings at that fare. On the early (GCR) issues the individual bookings were all named, those in one direction on one side of the ticket and those in the other on the opposite side. The last GCR and all LNER tickets followed a similar practice but with the pairs of bookings named once only in the form 'A and B'. The new

issues introduced with the BTC charges scheme in 1952 no longer named individual bookings but showed numbered punch spaces down each side, the number of punch spaces on each value corresponding to the number of pairs of bookings at each fare. (Note that these numbers were not fare stages as would be expected on a normal numbered tramway punch ticket.) Similar tickets, but with punch spaces down one side only, were used for the early morning returns introduced in 1952 and the special cheap days which replaced them in 1959. A feature of railway practice not met with on other tramways was the manuscript amendment of tickets to show new fares.

Workman's, military and privilege tickets are known from the GCR period and various other issues for throughout journeys from LNER days. These tickets were all printed for specific journeys and represented an adaption of standard railway tickets to the punch type format. Tickets in virtually identical layouts continued to be used for other than workman's returns into BR days and right up to the closure.

The "Tramway Station" at Corporation Bridge, 10 June 1956   [J C Gillham]

4 - Great Central Railway Tickets

Single Tickets

Single tickets of the GCR period are known in the following six styles, although some have only been seen as printers proofs and may thus have never actually been used:-

(1) Title in two lines **"GREAT CENTRAL RLY. / (Grimsby District Electric Rly.)"**; conditions reading up centre column; stages each side - in one direction on left, in the other on right; back blank or with commercial advertisement.

(2) As (1), but conditions reading down centre column.

(3) As (2), but title **"GREAT CENTRAL RLY. / Grimsby & Immingham Electric Rly"** (i.e. wording of second line different and now without brackets).

(4) As (3), but title **"Great Central Rly./Grimsby & Immingham Electric Rly"** (i.e. first line now in lower case).

(5) As (4), but conditions once again reading up centre column.

(6) Title as (4) except **"... Electric Ry"** in second line; conditions on back; stages shown once only, across centre of ticket.

Individual values/colours and the stages on them (in most cases much abbreviated) are:-

Type 1

1d	green	Corporation Bridge / Cleveland Bridge
		Cleveland Bridge / Great Coates Level Crossing
4d	green	Great Coates Level Crossing / Immingham
		Cleveland Bridge / Immingham
5d	blue	Grimsby Corporation Bridge / Immingham
6d	pale blue	Grimsby Corporation Bridge / Immingham Dock
8d	(see note)	Grimsby Corporation Bridge / Immingham Dock
		(One example is an unknown colour, another reported as buff with a vertical blue band. In view of the colour of the Type 2 issue, the latter may be faded)

These are all issued and apart from the 8d, represent the pre-1917 fare scale. The 8d is a 1917 fare. The tickets with just "Immingham" probably predate the opening to Immingham Dock in 1913.

Type 1

Type 2
Compare stages with those shown
on ticket J4645

Type 2

1d	green	Grimsby Corporation Bridge / Cleveland Bridge
		Cleveland Bridge / Great Coates Level Crossing
3d	white with vertical green band	Grimsby Corporation Bridge / Great Coates Level Crossing
		Cleveland Bridge / No.5 Passing Place
		Great Coates Level Crossing / Marsh Road Level Crossing
		No.5 Passing Place / Kiln Lane
		Marsh Road Level Crossing / Immingham Town

4d	drab	Immingham Dock / No.5 Passing Place
		Immingham Halt / Great Coates Level Crossing
		Immingham Halt / Cleveland Bridge
		Marsh Lane Level Crossing / Grimsby Corporation Bridge
		(note "Immingham Halt" and "Marsh Lane (actually "L" on the ticket) Level Crossing")
6d	lilac	Grimsby Corporation Bridge / Immingham Town
		No.5 Passing Place / Immingham Dock
8d	white	Grimsby Corporation Bridge / Immingham Dock
	with vertical	
	green band	

The 1d and 8d are issued, the others unissued but, apart from the 4d, "0000", have normal looking serial numbers. The 1d and 4d are pre-1917 fares, the remainder 1917 fares.

Type 3

1d	green	Grimsby Corporation Bridge / Cleveland Bridge
		Cleveland Bridge / Great Coates Level Crossing
		No.5 Passing Place / Marsh Road Level Crossing
		No.5 Passing Place / Great Coates Level Crossing
		Marsh Road Level Crossing / Kiln Lane Level Crossing
		Kiln Lane Level Crossing / Immingham Town
		Eastern Entrance / Immingham Dock
2d	lilac	Great Coates Level Crossing / Grimsby Corporation Bridge
		No.5 Passing Place / Cleveland Bridge
		Marsh Road Level Crossing / Great Coates Level Crossing
		Immingham Town / Marsh Road Level Crossing
		Immingham Dock / Kiln Lane Level Crossing
		No.5 Passing Place / Kiln Lane No.8
		Immingham Dock / Immingham Town
		(Note "Kiln Lane No.8")

Both these are printers proofs with serials "0000" and show pre-1917 fares. Probably proofs produced prior to the 1920 fare increase and with the fare not yet amended.

Type 4

3½d	white	Grimsby Corporation Bridge / Great Coates Level Crossing
	with	Stortford Street / Great Coates
	vertical	Great Coates / Marsh Road
	yellow	No.5 Passing Place / Kiln Lane
	band	Marsh Road / Immingham Town
		Immingham Town / Immingham Dock
9d	blue	Grimsby Corporation Bridge / Kiln Lane or Immingham Town
		Stortford Street / Kiln Lane or Immingham Town
		Cleveland Bridge / Immingham Dock
		Great Coates / Immingham Dock
10½d	lilac	Grimsby Corporation Bridge / Immingham Dock
		Stortford Street / Immingham Dock
10½d	lilac	Grimsby Corporation Bridge / Immingham Dock

Type 4

Type 5

Type 5

9d	blue	Grimsby Corporation Bridge / Kiln Lane or Immingham Town
		Stortford Street / Kiln Lane or Immingham Town
		Cleveland Bridge / Immingham Dock
		Great Coates / Immingham Dock

All the tickets of types 4 and 5 are issued, and clearly represent the 1920 fare scale.

Type 6

2d	blue	Grimsby Corporation Bridge to Cleveland Bridge
		Cleveland Bridge to Great Coates Level Crossing
		Great Coates Level Crossing to No.5 Passing Place
		No.5 Passing Place to Marsh Road Level Crossing
		Marsh Road Level Crossing to Kiln Lane
		Kiln Lane to Immingham Town
		Immingham Town to Immingham Dock
4d	white with vertical lilac band	Grimsby Corporation Bridge to No.5 Passing Place
		Cleveland Bridge to Marsh Road Level Crossing
		Great Coates Level Crossing to Kiln Lane
		No.5 Passing Place to Immingham Town
		Marsh Road Level Crossing to Immingham Dock
		("Marsh Road Level Crossing" is deleted from the last stage and "Kiln Lane" substituted in manuscript.)
5d	green	Grimsby Corporation Bridge to Marsh Road Level Crossing
		Cleveland Bridge to Immingham Town
		Marsh Road Level Crossing to Immingham Dock
7d	white	Cleveland Bridge to Immingham Dock

These are all unissued, but have normal serials so were probably used. They represent the only evidence of a reduction in fares, presumably at the beginning of 1923.

Other Types of Tickets

A number of GCR tickets other than singles have also been seen, although again many are unissued or printers proofs. The general style of most of these is similar, with the fare across the top of the centre column, type of ticket reading down this column (up in the case of (2) and (9), below) and the journey shown in one direction on the left, in the other direction on the right. Conditions appropriate to the type of ticket appear on the back. The night workman's ticket (1) has conditions reading up the centre column while the other workman's ticket (6) has them reading across the ticket, while both have punch spaces for the days of the week along the edges. The following have the earlier ("Grimsby District Electric Rly") title:-

(1) **3d** buff night workman's return Grimsby Corporation Bridge and Immingham Dock, with extensive conditions on the back (typical of railway workman's tickets of the period) limiting the company's liability.

(2) **Naval or Military** ticket issued in exchange for a warrant and showing (in the same style as the singles) stages:-
Grimsby Corporation Bridge / Immingham Dock
Stallingboro' (No.8 Loop) / Immingham Dock
Stallingboro' (No.8 Loop) / Grimsby Corporation Bridge

(3) **3d** white "S.P.T." (i.e. staff privilege ticket) return Immingham and Grimsby Corporation Bridge, with standard GCR privilege ticket conditions on the back.

(4) **3d** lilac dog single Grimsby Corporation Bridge and Immingham Dock.

(5) **6d** yellow bicycle single Grimsby Corporation Bridge and Immingham Dock.

All these probably represent the pre-1917 fare scale, while (3) seems likely to date from 1912/13, prior to the extension to Immingham Dock.

Other later tickets, all with the "Grimsby & Immingham Electric Rly" title are:-

(6) **8d** vertically bicoloured blue/white day workman's return Grimsby Corporation Bridge and Immingham Dock, again with typical workman's ticket conditions on the back.

(7) **8d** lemon naval or military return Grimsby Corporation Bridge and Immingham Dock.

(8) **4½d** buff "S.P.T." return Immingham Town and Grimsby Corporation Bridge similar to the earlier 3d issue.

(9) **3d** green folding mail cart single Grimsby Corporation Bridge and Immingham Dock.

Of these, (7) appears to be a 1917 fare, while the others are probably 1920 fares.

Night Workman's Return

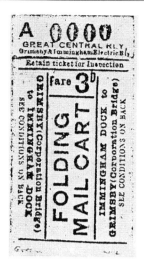

Naval or Military Return	Dog	Staff Privilege Ticket	Folding Mail Cart

Grimsby District Electric Railway title   Grimsby & Immingham Electric Rly title

Staff Free Pass

Finally, mention must be made of a printers proof of a GCR free pass identical in layout to the LNER issue described later, but on white card about 1½" deep and with serial numbers along the bottom on each half. Whether tickets in this form were ever actually produced, or whether the punch ticket format of the LNER issues was adopted is not known.

GRIMSBY AND IMMINGHAM ELECTRIC RAILWAY.

Grimsby (Corporation Bridge) to Immingham Dock.							Immingham Dock to Grimsby (Corporation Bridge).						
WEEK DAYS.				SUNDAYS.			WEEK DAYS.				SUNDAYS.		
Depart. a.m	Depart. a.m	Depart. p.m	Depart. p.m	Depart a.m	Depart p.m	Depa't p.m	Depart. a.m	Depart. a.m	Depart. p.m	Depart. p.m	Depart a.m	Depart p.m	Depart p.m
3A 0	8A 0	1 0	5Q40	3 0	1 20	9 40	12B25	9 40	1 30SO	5B30	12 25	1 0	7 0
5A15	8A20	1 20	5B53SX	5 20	1 40	10 20	3D47	10 0	1 40	5B40	3 47	1 20	7 40
5A20	8A30	1 40	6G 0	6 0	2 0	10 42	5D19	10 20	2 0	5B50SX	6 0	1 40	8 20
5A25	8A40	2 0	6G20	7 0	2 20	11 0	6D 0	10 40	2 20	6B 0	6 33	2 0	9 0
5A30	9A 0	2 20	6G40	7 6	2 40	11 50	6D28	11 0	2 40	6B20	7 0	2 20	9 40
5A50	9 20	2 40	7G20	7 50	3 0	.	6D35	11 20	3 0	6B40	7 40	2 40	10 12
6A 0	9 40	3 0	7G40SX	8 0	3 20	...	6D40	11 40	3 20	6B50SX	8 10	3 0	10 20
6A 5	10 0	3 20	8C 0	8 30	3 40	...	6D50	noon.	3 40	7B 0	8 30	3 20	11 15
6A13	10 20	3 40	8 40	9 0	4 0	...	7 0 0	12 0	3 55SX	7B20	9 0	3 40	...
6A20	10 40	4G 0	9 0	9 5	4 20	...	7G20	p.m.	4B 0	8B 0	9 40	4 0	...
6A25	11 0	4G18	9 20	9 40	5 0	...	7G40	12 10 SO	4B20	8B30SX	10 25	4 20	...
6A40	11 20	4C27SX	10 0	10 20	5 20	...	8 0 0	12 16SO	4B40	8B40	11 0	4 40	...
6A50	11 40	4G40	10 20	11 0	5 40	...	8D 5	12 20	4B50	9C20	11 40	5 0	...
7A 0	12 0	4G50	10 40	11 40	6 20	...	8D10	12 30 SO	5B 0	9B10	noon	5 10	...
7A15	p.m	4G58	11 20	p.m	7 0	...	8D25	12 40	5B 5	10G 0	12 0	5 20	...
7A20	12 20	5C15SX	.	12 20	7 40	...	8 40	1 0	5B10	10B10	p.m	5 40	...
7A28	12 27SO	5G20	...	12 40	8 20	...	9 0	1 10SO	5B15	11B20	12 20	6 0	...
7A50	12 40	5C25		1 0	9 0	.	9 20	1 20	5B20	.	12 40	6 20	...

This service is subject to revision. Particulars of any alterations made will be announced locally.
SO Saturdays only.   SX Saturdays excepted.

The Cars stop at the following places:—Yarboro' Street, Stortford Street, Cleveland Bridge and Immingham Town, and by request at Jackson Street, Boulevard Recreation Ground, Great Coates Level Crossing, Marsh Road Level Crossing, Kiln Lane (Stallingboro'), and Eastern entrance to Immingham Dock. Workmen's Daily Return Tickets, Grimsby to Immingham Dock, fare 3d., are issued to bona-fide workmen by Cars marked "A," available to return by Cars marked "B." Workmen's Nightly Return Tickets, Grimsby to Immingham Dock, fare 3d., are issued to bona-fide workmen by cars marked "C," available to return by cars marked "D." On Sats. only Workmen's Daily Return Tickets are available to return by any Car after 11.15 a.m.

From the Great Central Railway timetable dated 5th May 1919.
Note the reference to a stop at "Eastern entrance to Immingham Dock".

5 - Single Tickets - LNER Period

General Description

All the LNER single tickets seen from the Grimsby & Immingham are printed by Edmondson to the same basic design. This is clearly a development of the final GCR design (type 6) and differs from it only in the title and its arrangement. The company title appears as initials only ("**L.N.E.Ry**", later "**L.N.E.R.**"), with the sub-title "**Grimsby & Immingham ELECTRIC RAILWAY**" in four lines to the left of the fare and "RETAIN TICKET FOR INSPECTION" to the right. The stage names appear across the ticket, in the form "A & B" (the previous GCR issues had shown the journey in one direction only as "A to B"). Child tickets have a red overprint "CHILD" reading up the centre of the ticket. The colour schemes used often (particularly for child issues) include overprinted vertical bars (normally around 9mm wide but sometimes as wide as 12mm or as narrow as 7mm) or stripes (normally around 3mm wide, but on later issues only 1-1½mm wide). There is also much shade variation in the basic colours used. There were a few post-nationalisation tickets in the LNER design and these are, for convenience, included in this section.

Six styles of LNER single (plus one with BR title) can be identified by differences in heading, style of type (originally serif, later a very distinctive sans-serif) for stage detail and conditions on the back thus:-

Type	Heading	Stage Details	Back
A	"L.N.E.Ry"	serif	blank
B	"L.N.E.R."	serif	blank
C	"L.N.E.R."	serif	six lines of conditions, last line "Regulations & Bills"
D	"L.N.E.R."	sans-serif	six lines of conditions, last line "Regulations & Bills"
E	"L.N.E.R."	sans-serif	four lines of conditions, last line "Bills and Notices"
F	"L.N.E.R."	sans-serif	five lines of conditions, last line "and Notices"
G	"BRITISH RLYS. (E)"	sans-serif	five lines of conditions referring to Railway Executive.

In addition to these variations in the basic ticket, three different styles of child overprint are known:-

(a) large sans-serif letters in centre of ticket
(b) large serif letters in centre of ticket
(c) small sans-serif letters at bottom of ticket

Overprint (a) has been seen on a few issues of type B (child type Ba), (b) on types A,B and some C (child types Ab, Bb, Cb) and (c) on other type C and later types (child types Cc, etc.).

It is very difficult to date the different styles of ticket exactly. Certainly none are from the first year of the LNER (1923), since such tickets would have been expected to have the heading "L.& N.E.Ry", a title not seen on a Grimsby and Immingham single ticket. All the LNER single tickets seen are for the January 1928 fare scale or later. However, tickets for the street tramway section produced at about the time of the introduction of the local service in September 1928 are of type B and type A is clearly earlier than this. Thus, either types A and B were current in quick succession in 1928 or the "1928" fare scale is actually earlier than supposed. If this is the case, type A could perhaps date from as early as 1924/5, with type B in use by 1928. Type C is known to predate the 1937 fare increase, and was used for another new ticket for the street tramway section introduced some time after 1933 but before 1937. The few tickets of type D have "C" (1st December 1940) fares, while the revised conditions wording of type E is known on other LNER tickets from late 1940, thus these two types probably followed each other in quick succession in 1940/41. (It is perhaps worth commenting that the "...Timetables Bills and Notices" form of conditions wording used by the LNER for a short period in 1939/40 does not seem to have appeared on any Grimsby & Immingham ticket.) Type F is probably late LNER or even posthumous. Type G will date from some time after the first use of the BR title on tickets in 1950, and will have been used up to the introduction of the new style BR tickets in 1952.

The main range of LNER single tickets probably originally consisted of ten adult and ten child tickets (although three of the latter have not been seen), covering between them all possible adult and child bookings on the main part of the line. In addition, the tickets covering bookings from Corporation Bridge also included (at the same fare) the corresponding booking from an intermediate point on the street tramway section. This was originally Stortford Street, but with new tickets produced for the 1937 fare increase (and later) Beeson Street was used instead. The reason for this practice is not known, but it would appear to have been unnecessary duplication of stages. The main range of tickets was supplemented by a small number of tickets covering bookings local to the street tramway section.

It seems probable that with the introduction of the "1928" fare scale (which may actually have come into use earlier than this) a full set of ten adult and ten child tickets (together with tickets for whatever local bookings then applied on the street tramway section) were produced in type A. Subsequent reprints for all but the least used adult tickets and several of the child tickets, as well as new tickets required for changes in the street tramway fare scale were later produced in type B, with one or two late examples in type C. With the 1937 fare increase reprints in type C were provided for all ten adult tickets, most of the child tickets and the street tramway tickets. Three of the child tickets are not recorded, but there is clear evidence that, at the time of the 1937 revision, two of these were eliminated by modifying stages on other tickets and the third was probably eliminated in the same way. After 1937, there was clearly no complete reprinting of tickets and stocks were used up with fares amended in manuscript. The few heavily used bookings were, however, reprinted frequently and progressed through types C, D and E during the C fare scale period. The few P and Z fare scale tickets were in types E and F and (right at the end of this period) type G.

The individual tickets will now be considered in detail in three groups - the main range of ten adult tickets, the ten corresponding child tickets and the tickets for the street tramway section. In the first two groups tickets were in the same colours throughout although successive printings were in the different types detailed above and had revised fares as appropriate. In most cases stages did not change apart from on some of the child tickets, details of which are given in the lists which follow. However, there were two general changes to stage names:-

(a)   the replacement of Stortford Street by Beeson Street in 1937 already mentioned.

(b)   tickets of type A (only) used the name "Corporation Bridge" (without Grimsby), rather than "Grimsby Corp. Bridge" as used on all later types.

Tickets for local journeys on the street tramway section were, because of changes to the fare stages, much more complicated. The chapter on fares sets out the three distinct fare scales which seem likely to have been used up to 1937, and the tickets will be dealt with in relation to the periods of these fare scales as follows:-

Period 1 - up to about 1928/9.
Period 2 - 1928/9 to the mid 1930s.
Period 3 - mid 1930s to 1937.
Period 4 - "N" fare scale and later.

Within each group tickets will be given an identification number or letter and the stages and colours noted, together with any changes or other significant information. Individual printings and the fares shown on them will be shown in tables at the end of this section.

Adult Tickets - Main Range

(1)   Colour - buff, showing stages:-
> Grimsby Corp. Bridge & Cleveland Bridge
> Cleveland Bridge & Gt. Coates L. Crossing
> Gt. Coates L. Crossing & No.5 Passing Place
> No.5 Passing Place & Marsh Rd. L. Crossing
> Marsh Rd. L. Crossing & Kiln Lane L. Crossing
> Kiln Lane L. Crossing & Immingham Town

(2)   Colour - salmon, two vertical red stripes (later printings narrow stripes), showing stages:-
> Grimsby Corp. Bridge & Gt. Coates L. Crossing
> Stortford Street/Beeson Street & Gt. Coates L. Crossing
> Cleveland Bridge & No.5 Passing Place
> No.5 Passing Place & Kiln Lane L. Crossing
> Marsh Rd. L. Crossing & Immingham Town
> Immingham Town & Immingham Dock

(3)   Colour - orange, two vertical green stripes, showing stage:-
> Gt. Coates L. Crossing AND Marsh Rd. L. Crossing

(4)   Colour - white, showing stage:-
> Kiln Lane L. Crossing AND Immingham Dock

(5)   Colour - dark blue, showing stages:-
> Grimsby Corp. Bridge & No.5 Passing Place
> Stortford Street/Beeson Street & No.5 Passing Place
> Cleveland Bridge & Marsh Rd. L. Crossing
> Gt. Coates L. Crossing & Kiln Lane L. Crossing
> No.5 Passing Place & Immingham Town

(6)   Colour - dark blue, two vertical red stripes, showing stage:-
> Marsh Rd. L. Crossing AND Immingham Dock

(7)   Colour - green, showing stages:-
> Grimsby Corp. Bridge & Marsh Rd. L. Crossing
> Stortford Street/Beeson Street & Marsh Rd. L. Crossing
> Gt. Coates L. Crossing AND Immingham Town
> No.5 Passing Place & Immingham Dock

(8)   Colour - lemon, showing stages:-
> Cleveland Bridge AND Kiln Lane L. Crossing
> Cleveland Bridge AND Immingham Town

(9)   Colour - light blue, showing stages:-
> Grimsby Corp. Bridge & Kiln Lane L. Crossing
> Grimsby Corp. Bridge & Immingham Town
> Stortford Street/Beeson Street & Kiln Lane L. Crossing
> Stortford Street/Beeson Street & Immingham Town
> Cleveland Bridge & Immingham Dock
> Gt. Coates L. Crossing & Immingham Dock

(10)   Colour - magenta, (earlier tickets which look grey could well be faded) showing stages:-
> Grimsby Corp. Bridge AND Immingham Dock
> Stortford Street/Beeson Street AND Immingham Dock

(1) (2) (2) (3)

(3) (4) (5) (6)

(7) (8) (9) (10)

Adult Tickets - Main Range

Child Tickets - Main Range

(1C) Colour - buff, showing stages as adult ticket (1).

(2C) Colour - magenta, vertical green bar, showing stages as adult ticket (2). Later printings have an additional stage added to replace ticket (3C):-

Gt. Coates L. Crossing & Marsh Rd. L. Crossing

(3C) Not seen, but booking later covered by ticket (2C) above.

(4C) Colour - white, vertical red bar, showing stage as adult ticket (4).

(5C) Colour - salmon, three vertical blue stripes, showing stages as adult ticket (5).

(6C) Not seen.

(7C) Colour - green, vertical red bar, showing stages as adult ticket (7), plus:-

Stortford Street & Immingham Town

This must have been a printing error, since this stage appeared on both adult ticket (9) and its child equivalent (9C). On a later printing it was deleted and an additional stage added to replace ticket (8C):-

Cleveland Bridge & Immingham Town

(8C) Not seen, but booking later covered by ticket (7C) above.

(9C) Colour - yellow, vertical red bar, showing stages as adult ticket (9), but omitting Corporation Bridge/Kiln Lane and Beeson Street/Kiln Lane. This would cause no problems as these stages were covered by Corporation Bridge/Beeson Street - Immingham Town. The mystery is why these stages appeared separately on the adult ticket, and indeed why Beeson Street stages were shown at all, since they duplicated Corporation Bridge!

(10C) Colour - magenta, vertical red bar, showing stages as adult ticket (10).

(1C)

(2C)

(2C)

(4C)

(5C)

(7C)

(9C)

(10C)

Child Tickets - Main Range

Street Tramway Tickets - Period 1

The Corporation Bridge/Cleveland Bridge booking will have been covered by the 2½d adult and 1½d child (tickets (1) and (1C)) in the main range, with one additional adult ticket for intermediate bookings:-

(A)   **1½d** pink showing stages:-

Grimsby Corp. Bridge & Stortford Street
Stortford Street & Cleveland Bridge

There is also likely to have been a 1d child ticket covering the same stages, although this has not been seen.

Street Tramway Tickets - Period 2

Ticket (A), its presumed child equivalent and the Corporation Bridge/Cleveland Bridge stage on tickets (1) and (1C) replaced by a new set of three adult and two child tickets covered all bookings local to the street tramway:-

(B)   **1d** grey showing stages:-

Grimsby Corp. Bridge & Beeson Street
Beeson Street & Spencer Street

(C)   **1½d** yellow-green, two vertical green stripes   }

(D)   **1d child** yellow-green, vertical green bar   }
        both showing stages:-

Grimsby Corp. Bridge AND Spencer Street
Spencer Street AND Cleveland Bridge
Cleveland Bridge AND Beeson Street

(E)   **2d** orange with two vertical green stripes   }

(F)   **1d child** orange, vertical green bar   }
        both showing stage:-

Grimsby Corp. Bridge AND Cleveland Bridge

It is not clear why two separate 1d child tickets were considered necessary, but the similarity of both colours and stages to the corresponding adult tickets seem to indicate that they belong here.

Street Tramway Tickets - Period 3

Tickets (C) and (E) remained in use, but ticket (B) and the first stage on ticket (C) were replaced by a new ticket:-

(G)   **1d** orange, vertical green bar flanked by two narrow (1mm) vertical green stripes, showing stage:-

Grimsby Corp. Bridge To Cleveland Street

No new child ticket seems to have been provided, probably the existing tickets (D) and/or (F) were used.

Street Tramway Tickets - Period 4

Ticket (G) remained in use after the introduction of the "N" fares, but with the fare increased to 1½d. Tickets (E) and (F) were replaced once again by the Corporation Bridge/Cleveland Bridge stage on tickets (1) and (1C) in the main set. The intermediate bookings were catered for by two new tickets produced by modifying the stages on tickets (C) and (F):-

(H)   **1½d** yellow-green, two vertical green stripes showing stages:-

Cleveland Street AND Cleveland Bridge
Cleveland Bridge AND Beeson Street

(I)   **1d child** orange, vertical green bar showing stages:-

Grimsby Corp. Bridge AND Cleveland Street
Beeson Street AND Cleveland Bridge

With subsequent fare changes, these three tickets took the appropriate scale increases.

(F)

(G)

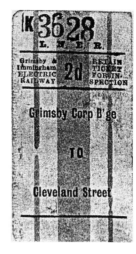

(G)

(H)

(I)

**Street Tramway
Tickets**

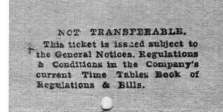

Type C and D:
".... Regulations & Bills"

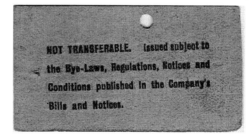

Type E:
".... Bills and Notices"

Type F:
".... and Notices"

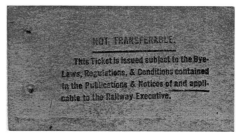

Type G:
reference to ".... Railway Executive"

Backs - all types

Ticket Types and Values

Adult Tickets (1) to (10)

Type	Fare Scale	1	2	3	4	5	6	7	8	9	10
A	1928	2½d	a	a	4½d	a	6d	a	7½d	a	a
B	1928	2½d	3d	3½d	b	5½d	b	7d	b	9d	10½d
											c
C	1928	d	.	.	.	.	.	.	.	.	10½d
		h									
C	N	2½d	3½d	4d	5d	6d	6½d	7½d	8d	9½d	11d
		g	g	g	e				e	f	f
C	R	.	.	.	(6d)*	7d*	7½d*	8½d*	(9d)*	(10½d)	(1/-)
		g		e	g	g	g	g	g		
C	C	.	4½d	(5d)*	.	.	.	.	.	11½d*	1/1*
D	C	.	4½d						.	11½d	1/1
E	C	2½d	4½d	.	.	.	.	.	.	11½d	.
			g	g	e	e	e	e	e	f	f
E	P	3½d*	.	.	(7d)	(8d)	(8½d)	(10½d)	(11d)	(1/0½d)	(1/3)*
			g	e	e	e	e	e	e		
E	Z	.	5½d*	(6d)	(8d)	(9d)*	(10½d)*	(11½d)	(1/-)	(1/2½)*	1/5*
F	Z	.	5½d	.	.	.	.	.	.	.	1/5
G	Z	.	5½d	.	.	.	.	.	.	.	1/5

Child Tickets (1C) to (10C)

Type	Fare Scale	1C	2C	3C	4C	5C	6C	7C	8C	9C	10C
				i			j		i		
Ab	1928	a	a	(2d)	2½d	3d	(3d)	3½d	(4d)	a	5½d
Bb	1928	.	1½d	.	.	.	.	b	.	4½d	.
		g			g	g					g
Cb	N	1½d	2d	.	.	.	.	4d	.	5d	.
Cc	N	1½d	2d	.	.	3d	.	.	.	5d	5½d
		g	g		e	e		f		f	f
-	R	.	.	.	(3d)*	(3½d)*	.	(4½d)*	.	(5½d)	(6d)
		g	g		e	e		g		e	e
Cc	C	.	2½d	.	.	.	.	.	.	(6d)*	(6½d)*
Ec	C	.	2½d	.	.	.	.	.	.	.	.
		e	g		e	e		f		e	e
-	P	(2d)*	.	.	(3½d)	(4d)	.	(5½d)	.	(6½d)	(7½d)
		g			e	e		e		e	e
	Z	.	(3d)	.	(4d)	(4½d)*	.	(6d)*	.	(7½d)	(8½d)
Gc	Z	.	3d	.	.	.	.	.	.	.	.

Street Tramway Tickets (A) to (I)

Type	Fare Scale	A	B	C	D	E	F	G	H	I
B	Period 1	1½d	.	.	.	.	.	.	.	.
B	Period 2	.	1d	1½d	.	2d	.	.	.	.
Ba	Period 2	.	.	.	1d	.	1d	.	.	.
C	Period 3	.	.	l	k	k	l	1d	.	.
C	N/R/C	.	.	.	.	.	.	1½d	2d	.
Cb		.	.	.	.	.	.	.	.	1d
Cc		.	.	.	.	.	.	.	.	1d
D		.	.	.	.	.	.	1½d	.	.
E		.	.	.	.	.	.	1½d	.	.
Ec		.	.	.	.	.	.	.	.	1d
E	P	.	.	.	.	.	.	2d*	(2½d)*	.
G	Z	.	.	.	.	.	.	2½d*	(3d)	(1½d)*

Notes:

1d Value known to exist in this type.

(6d) New fare for which no ticket has been seen.

* Example seen of ticket at earlier fare amended in manuscript to cover this fare.

a Complete set of tickets in types A/Ab probably produced in early LNER days, so value likely to exist.

b Set of tickets amended in manuscript as specimens for printing of new "N" scale tickets seen. Ticket used for this value is type A/Ab, so type B/Bb probably does not exist.

c Only type C ticket with earlier stage name Stortford Street.

d Printing of this ticket without Corporation Bridge/Cleveland Bridge stage should exist, but no example yet seen.

e Fare changed at this point, but no ticket at this fare seen.

f Fare changed at this point, but ticket for previous fare seen amended in manuscript for later fare, so ticket at this fare probably does not exist.

g Fare did not change at this point.

h Fare did not change at this point, but fare Corporation Bridge/Cleveland Bridge once again 2½d and covered by this ticket.

i Booking not otherwise provided for, so ticket probably existed in type Ab. Covered by addition to another ticket from 1937.

j Booking not otherwise provided for at any stage, so ticket probably existed at least in type Ab.

k Probably remained in use, but no later print seen.

l Probably remained in use; example used as specimen for new "N" fare tickets is type B, so later print unlikely to exist.

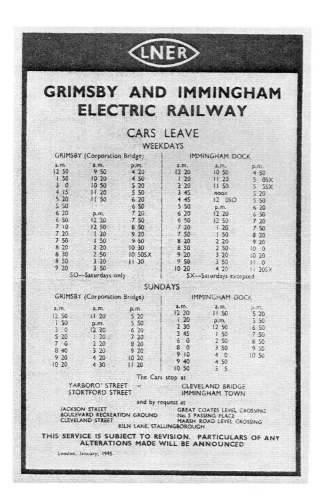

LNER. timetable - January 1945

GREAT CENTRAL RAILWAY

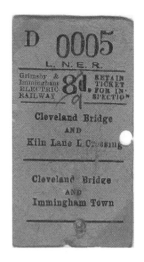

L. N. E. R.

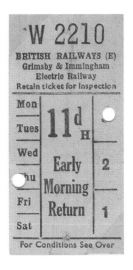

Harland of Hull   Bell Punch Co.

Bell Punch Co.

Williamson

BRITISH RAILWAYS

6 - Workman's Tickets - LNER Period

General Description

As befits a line built primarily for carriage of workmen to the new docks at Immingham, workman's tickets survive in profusion and, for the common bookings, obviously had to be reprinted quite frequently. This means that there are many detailed variations between individual printings. However, all these tickets from the LNER period (and BR tickets in LNER style, again included here for convenience) were by Edmondson to the same general design with conditions on both front and back and punch spaces along the edges for the days of the week. Some tickets were printed, for example, "Grimsby (Corp'n Bridge) and Immingham Dock", and were obviously issued in either direction while others read, for example, "Immingham Town to Gt. Coates Level C." and were presumably only issued in the direction stated. The standard colour for workman's tickets was vertically bicoloured blue and white on the front with a white back, the blue being on the right at first, but on the left later. One ticket (Cleveland Bridge/Immingham Town) is buff with two vertical brown stripes, but it is not clear whether this represents some special facility or an earlier practice.

There were six different front layouts used for workman's tickets during the LNER and early BR period (to 1952). These are:-

(1)   Heading "L.N.E.R."; nine lines of conditions on front referring to "Specified Tram-Cars", last line "pany's Bills and Notices."; "FARE" in capitals and above fare value.
(2)   Conditions slightly reset, last line now "Notices."
(3)   Conditions now refer to "Special Tram-Cars"

and extended to read "... Bye-laws Regulations, Notices and conditions published in the Company's Bills and Notices.".
(4)   Conditions wording reverts to that of (1) and (2), but referring to "Special Tram-Cars" and last line now "and Notices."; "Fare" now in lower case type and on same line as fare value.
(5)   Conditions reset, last line "Bills and Notices.".
(6)   Heading "BRITISH RAILWAYS (E)", but conditions as (5) and still refer to "Company".

With these fronts were six different backs with conditions as follows:-

(1)   Lengthy workman's conditions limiting company's liability to £100.
(2)   Four lines, last line "Bills and Notices".
(3)   Five lines, last line "and Notices".
(4)   Six lines, last line "Railway Executive".
(5)   Six lines, last line "Executive".
(6)   Five lines, last line "..cable to the Railway Executive"

Dating these changes is not easy, but it seems likely that the front (1)/back (1) combination was in use from early LNER days until around 1940, the blue colour moving from right to left over a period from the late 1930s. Front (2) (with backs (1), then (2)), front (3) (with back (1), then blank back) and front (4)/back (2) seem to have followed in quick succession in the early 1940s. Back (3), at first with front (4), then front (5), probably dates from just 1948/9 and front (6) (with backs (4), then (5) and (6)) from 1950/52.

Individual Tickets

Journey	Fare	Scale	Front	Back	Blue
Corporation Br & Cleveland Br	2d	1928/N/R/C	1	1	right
	2d		1	1	left
Corporation Br/Great Coates (a)	4½dZ	Z	6	4	left
Corporation Br & Immingham Town	6½d	1928/N	1	1	right
	6½d		1	1	left
	7d	R/C	1	1	left
	7d		4	2	left
	10d	Z	4	?	left
	10dZ		4	?	left
	10dZ		5	3	left
	10dZ		6	4	left
	10dZ		6	6	left
Corporation Br & Immingham Dock	7½d	1928/N	1	1	right
	8½d	R/C	1	1	left
	8½d		2	1	left
	8½d		2	2	left
	8½d		3	1	left
	8½d		3	blank	left
	8½d		4	2	left
	9½d	P	4	2	left
	11½d	Z	4	2	left
	11½dZ		4	3	left
	11½dZ		5	3	left
	11½dZ		6	4	left
	11½dZ		6	5	left
Cleveland Br/Immingham Town (a)	6½d		1	1	(b)
Great Coates & Immingham Dock	6½d	R/C	2	1	left

Immingham Town to Great Coates	4½d	1928/N	1	1	right
	5d	R/C	1	1	right
	5d		1	1	left
	5d		2	1	left
	5d		4	2	left
Immingham Dock to Great Coates	6d	1928/N	1	1	right
	6½d	R/C	1	1	right
	6½d		4	2	left
	9½d	Z	(c)		

Notes

(a) ticket not seen by present writer, so not clear whether journey is shown in form "&" or "to".

(b) non-standard colour, buff, two vertical brown stripes.

(c) earlier ticket seen amended in manuscript as sample to printer for type 6 issue with this fare, but actual ticket not seen.

Front 1
"Specified Tram-Cars",
last line:
"....pany's Bills and Notices"

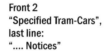

Front 2
"Specified Tram-Cars",
last line:
".... Notices"

Front 4
"Special Tram-Cars",
last line:
".... and Notices"

Front 5
last line:
".... Bills and Notices"

Front 6
heading: BRITISH RAILWAYS (E)

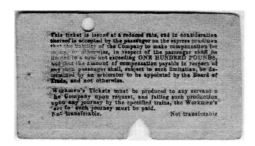

Back 1
Lengthy conditions

Back 2
Four-line conditions
last line: "... Bills and Notices"

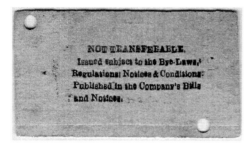

Back 3
Five-line conditions
last line: "... and Notices"

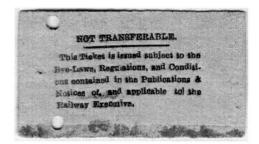

Back 4
Six-line conditions
last line: "... Railway Executive"

Edmondson Card Tickets

In addition to the punch type workman's tickets, three Edmondson card tickets for the Corporation Bridge/ Immingham Dock journey have been seen. One is a daily ticket, fare 8½d, vertically printed in roughly type 2 layout on white card with a central blue band and blank back. No issued examples are known but, as well as a specimen ticket with serials "0000", one example exists with a normal serial. This suggests that these tickets were produced for use, perhaps as a result of some wartime emergency (the fare is cor-

rect for the early 1940s), even if they were never actually used. The other two Edmondson cards are weekly workman's tickets, vertically printed in a similar layout to the Edmondson daily ticket, with standard LNER "Bills and Notices" conditions on the back. One is a six day ticket, on red card, and the other a seven day ticket, on blue card. Both are issued, dated with a rubber stamp (with 1945 dates) and have the weekly season ticket code number stamped on the front.

Pleasure Party One Day Return

Apart from the singles and workman's returns already covered, tickets of several other types were available for the full journey from Grimsby to Immingham Dock or to Immingham Town. One early ticket in this category is a "Pleasure Party One Day Return" to Immingham Town. This is vertically bicoloured buff and green (with green on the right) and is the only Grimsby & Immingham ticket seen with the very early form of company title "L.& N.E.RLY". It has the pencilled date 9/7/23 on the back, which is credible in view of the early form of title. Nothing is known of the facility this ticket represents, although possible uses have been discussed earlier, and the suggestion that it is a predecessor of the cheap returns disputed.

Cheap Returns

There is known to have been a cheap return fare between Grimsby and Immingham from early LNER days and quite a few tickets for this facility are known. As with the workman's tickets there were frequent reprints and detailed changes between different printings. All are vertically bicoloured green and white on the front (with green always on the left), white on the back. There are punch spaces for the days of the week down each side, availability at the top followed by the journey expressed as "Grimsby Corp. B. to Immingham Town or Dock and Vice Versa", conditions and fare. The back is blank. Child tickets have a vertical red overprint "CHILD", types (b) and (c), as described in the section on single tickets, being known. Types recorded are:-

(1)   Title "L.N.E.Rly"; availability between 9am and 4pm outward, between 10am and 4pm or after 7pm return; "Fare" in large lower case letters.

(2)   Title now "L.N.E.R"; availability outward after 9am, return by any car.

(3)   "FARE" now in smaller capital letters.

(4)   Availability outward after 7.45am, return by any car

(5)   Completely reset with same wording, but better spaced.

(6)   Journey shown as "Corporation Bridge and Immingham Dock"; conditions reset to end "Co's Bills & Notices".

Tickets known to exist are:-

Type (1)	1/- adult,	
	6d child (overprint (b))	
Type (2)	1/- adult	
		(base fare)
Type (3)	1/- adult	
	1/1 adult,	
	6½d child (overprint (b))	
Type (4)	1/1 adult	N fare
	6½d child (overprint (c))	
Type (5)	1/1 adult	
	1/2 adult	R fare
	1/3 adult	C fare
	7½d child (overprint (c))	C fare
Type (6)	1/8 adult	Z fare

The cheap return fare will have been withdrawn in 1942, during the currency of the C fare of 1/3, and replaced by a monthly return at 1/6 (see below). Examples of the 1/3 adult ticket (type 5) and the 6½d child ticket (type 4) have been seen with fares amended in manuscript to 1/6 and 9d, indicating that the cheap tickets were used up as monthly returns. The cheap fare was reintroduced after the war but the date is not known. The only postwar ticket seen is the adult for the Z fare, although a child ticket might be expected to exist.

Type 1
Title: L.N.E.Rly
"Fare" in lower-case

Type 3
Title: L.N.E.R.
"Fare" in smaller capital letters

Type 4
Availability: outward after
7.45am, return by any car

Type 5
Availability reset

Monthly Returns

The tickets at monthly return fare introduced on withdrawal of the cheap return were similar in design and colour to those they replaced, differences being the heading "RETURN TICKET", absence of any reference to availability and the journey details, which were now "Grimsby Corp B'ge to Immingham Dock and vice versa". Nowhere was there any indication that the ticket was a monthly return, although they are so described on a January 1945 handbill. Later printings of these tickets had the conditions removed from the front and standard four line conditions ending "Bills and Notices" added on the back. The first monthly returns had fare 1/6 (C fare), those in the later style had fares of 1/6, 1/8 (P fare) and 1/11 (Z fare), while the last printing had the later five line back ending "and Notices" and showed the fare as 1/11Z (also known amended to 2/2 for the post 1952 ordinary return). As mentioned above, child cheap returns were used up at the child monthly return fare but a 9d child monthly return in the earlier style with overprint type (c) was also produced.

C Fare

C Fare

Z Fare

Later back with
four-line conditions

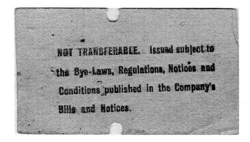

32

Forces Tickets

During the war there were many military establishments in the Grimsby area and provision seems to have been made for forces tickets while N fares were still in force, i.e. prior to 1st May 1940. Forces duty tickets were blue-green and forces leave tickets vertically bicoloured pink and white on the front (pink always on the left) and white on the back. The layout was as for the monthly returns, in two versions - (1) with conditions on the front and a blank back, (2) with standard four line conditions on the back. Tickets recorded are shown in the table below:-

Journey	Fare	Scale	Layout
"Service, Military, etc." (duty) single			
"Grimsby Corp. B'ge to Immingham Town or Dock"	-	-	(1)
"Service, Military, etc." (duty) return			
"Grimsby Corp. B'ge to Immingham Town or Dock and back"	-	-	(1)
"Furlough" (leave) single			
"Grimsby Corp. B'ge AND Immingham Dock"	7d	N	(1)
"Grimsby Corp. B'ge AND Immingham Dock"	7d	N	(2)
"Grimsby Corp. B'ge AND Immingham Dock"	8d	R	(2)
"Army and Navy on Leave" return			
"Grimsby Corp. B'ge to Immingham Town or Dock"	11d	N	(1)
"Grimsby Corp. B'ge to Immingham Town or Dock"	1/-	R	(1)
"Grimsby Corp. B'ge to Immingham Town or Dock"	1/1	C	(1)
"Grimsby Corp. B'ge AND Immingham Dock"	1/1	C	(1)
"Grimsby Corp. B'ge AND Immingham Dock"	1/1	C	(2)

Service, Military etc
"...Town or Dock"

Service, Military etc
"...Town or Dock and back"

Army and Navy on leave
Back blank

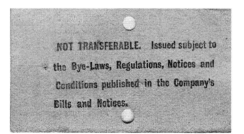

Army and Navy on leave
Conditions on back

Staff Free Pass

Staff travelling on duty used white horizontally printed two-coupon tickets with typical free pass conditions on the back. On the front was an instruction that the ticket was to be presented whole to the guard, who would return one half to the passenger. (Note the use of the term "guard", rather than "conductor".) These passes were presumably issued to men at their depots, to be handed to the conductor when they travelled.

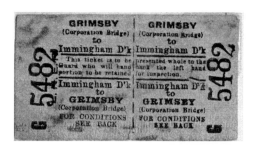

Privilege Tickets

Serving as it did the railway community of Immingham, it is to be expected that there would be many off-duty railwaymen and their families travelling on the line. For their use privilege returns between Immingham and Grimsby were provided. These were distinctive in design, with the journey shown in one direction along one edge of the ticket and in the opposite direction along the other edge. Special Privilege ticket conditions appeared on the back. Tickets known are:-

Corporation Bridge/Immingham Town
    Colour - light blue, two vertical brown stripes (later printings, marked *, with narrow stripes)
    Values - **4½d** (base fare), **5d** (N fare), **6d*** (C fare), **6½d*** (P fare), **7½d** (Z fare)
Corporation Bridge/Immingham Dock
    Colour - lilac, two vertical blue stripes (later printings, marked *, with narrow stripes)
    Values - **5½d** (base & N fares), **6d** (R fare), **6½d*** (C fare)
Corporation Bridge/Immingham Dock child
    Colour - blue, vertical brown bar and red "CHILD" overprint (both type (b) and type (c) on 3d; type (c) on 3½d)
    Values - **3d** (base, N & R fares), **3½d** (C fare)

The absence of separate child tickets for Immingham Town, which would appear to be the more likely journey, is surprising. The child fare for this journey would have been ½d cheaper than to Immingham Dock in all except the R fare scale.

Corporation Bridge /
Immingham Town
broad vertical bars

Corporation Bridge /
Immingham Town
narrow vertical bars

Corporation Bridge /
Immingham Dock
broad vertical bars

Corporation Bridge /
Immingham Dock
Child

Privilege back

Accompanied Traffic

The final tickets to be mentioned are those for accompanied animals and articles. These were similar in layout to the privilege tickets and had the appropriate article ticket conditions on the back. Rates were those applying for 10 miles, covering journeys from Grimsby to both Immingham Town and Dock, the tickets normally being printed for the latter journey. They do not make it clear whether they are singles or returns, but may well have been issued for either - in all cases the single and return rates were the same. Surprisingly no provision seems to have been made for articles accompanying privilege ticket holders (it was in BR days), for whom a lower rate should have applied. Surely wives of railwaymen from Immingham would have travelled into Grimsby with prams on occasions! The following tickets are known:-

Dog - Corporation Bridge/Immingham Town
    Colour - purple
    Value - **3d**
    This covers base, N and R rates, but it is not clear why the ticket is printed to Immingham Town only - the same rate would have applied to Immingham Dock.
Dog - Corporation Bridge/Immingham Dock
    Colour - purple
    Value - **4d** (C,P rate)
Bicycle or perambulator - Corporation Bridge/Immingham Dock
    Colour - yellow
    Values - **6d** (base, N rate), **7d** (R,C rate), **8d** (P rate), **9d** (Z rate), **11d** (A rate; BR(E) titled)
    Ticket also seen amended in manuscript for 1/1d rate.
Perambulator - Corporation Bridge/Immingham Dock
    Colour - light orange
    Value - **1/-**
    This ticket is rather a mystery. It is presumably for the B rate of April 1951, but it is not clear why it is for a pram only (earlier LNER and later BR issues were all for pram and bicycle). Also, if it were as late as 1951, it would have been expected to have had BR, rather than LNER, title.

Dog

Bicycle or Perambulator

Bicycle or Perambulator

Perambulator

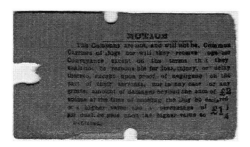

Back - Dog

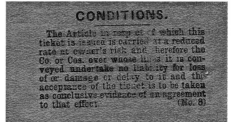

Back - Perambulator

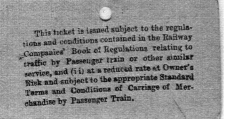

Back - Bicycle or Perambulator

8 - Single, Early Morning Return and Special Cheap Day Tickets - Post 1952

The radical change in the fares structure with the 1952 Charges Scheme resulted in, for all practical purposes, the introduction of a completely new range of tickets. These differed from their GCR and LNER counterparts in not showing geographical stages, but what appear at first sight to be stage numbers. In fact, however, they are best described as "booking numbers", each number representing a particular booking at the fare covered by the ticket concerned. The 2d single ticket of 1952 shows numbers 1 to 5 on each side and examination of the 1952 fare scale shows that there were five different 2d bookings - Corporation Bridge/Cleveland Street, Beeson Street or Cleveland Street/Cleveland Bridge, Cleveland Bridge/Great Coates, Marsh Road/Kiln Lane and Kiln Lane/Immingham Town. Thus, while we do not know for certain the actual punching arrangements, it seems reasonable to assume that a ticket issued from Corporation Bridge to Cleveland Street will have been punched in, say, "1" on one side of the ticket and so on up to "5" for a ticket issued from Kiln Lane to Immingham Town. Tickets issued in the reverse direction will presumably have been punched in the corresponding numbers on the opposite side of the ticket.

The early morning returns (and the special cheap days of 1959) were similar, but they only had one set of numbers, on the right hand side, the left hand side being taken up by punch spaces for days of the week. These tickets were punched in the day of the week and in a number, presumably indicating the journey in the same way as the singles. There does not appear to have been any way of indicating the direction of the outward journey, and thus nothing to prevent the ticket being used for two journeys in the same direction. It was presumably considered more important to ensure that tickets were not used to return other than on the day of issue (although there was nothing to prevent their use exactly a week later). It is understood that tickets issued to shift workers (under the standard railway arrangements) were punched in the serial number as well as the day of the week to indicate their validity for return on the day following that of issue, and a number of tickets have been seen so punched. Surprisingly there is no evidence that early morning return (or special cheap day) tickets were cancelled on the return journey.

Another notable feature of the post 1952 period is the use of more than one printer - after forty years of tickets by Edmondson, the nine years from 1952 to 1961 saw tickets first from Harland, then from Bell Punch and Williamson! This was in line with BR practice elsewhere with punch tickets, which were produced by Bell Punch and then Williamson during the 1950s. The use of Harland was, however, less usual, the only other BR use of this printer being for a few fixed value excess fare tickets. It is tempting to suggest that the use of Harland (a fairly local printer) in 1952 may have resulted from a need to obtain supplies quickly following late finalisation of details of the Charges Scheme (which certainly was the subject of much political argument just prior to its implementation). Details of the individual printings of tickets are listed below in relation to the changes in fares which led to their introduction.

1st May 1952 (singles)/1st September 1952 (EMRs)

Full range of single, child single and early morning return tickets by Harland to cover the new fares introduced with the BTC Charges Scheme. Singles were a dark blueish green, child singles had a diagonal (top left to bottom right) skeleton child overprint in red and early morning returns were white. All had brief conditions referring to the Railway Executive on the back with the heading "British Railways" and validity "Valid Day of Issue" on singles, "Valid as Dated by Authorised Trams" on early morning returns. All had the fare scale letter "H" after the fare. Individual tickets were:-

2d	single	booking numbers 1-5
4d	single	booking numbers 1-5
6d	single	booking numbers 1-5
7d	single	booking numbers 1-4
9d	single	booking numbers 1-3
11d	single	booking numbers 1-2
1/1	single	booking number 1
1d	child single	booking numbers 1-5
2d	child single	booking numbers 1-5
3d	child single	booking numbers 1-5
3½d	child single	booking numbers 1-4
4½d	child single	booking numbers 1-3
5½d	child single	booking numbers 1-2
6½d	child single	booking number 1
8d	early morning return	booking numbers 1-5
11d	early morning return	booking numbers 1-3
1/-	early morning return	booking numbers 1-2
1/2	early morning return	booking number 1

4d, 6d and 9d early morning returns should also exist, but have not been seen.

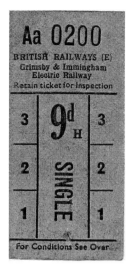

above: back - Singles

below: back - EMRs

1 May 1952 (Singles)
1 September 1952 (EMRs)
Printer: Harland
Title: BRITISH RAILWAYS (E)

Early 1953

As reprints of the original tickets were required, they were produced by Bell Punch to the same design, but with a distinctly different "look" to them because of the different printer. The most noticeable differences were the colour of the singles (a lighter, less blue, green), the child overprints (now diagonal bottom left to top right) and the addition of the printers imprint and block number. The backs had the same wording as the Harland prints, but now showed block numbers A3863 (singles) or A3862 (early morning returns). Individual tickets known are:-

2d	single	booking numbers	block H1480
4d	single	booking numbers 1-5	block H1481
6d	single	booking numbers 1-5	block H1482
9d	single	booking numbers 1-3	block H0718
11d	single	booking numbers 1-2	block H0719
11d	single	booking numbers 1-2	block H1484
2d	child single	booking numbers 1-5	block H1480
4d	early morning return	booking number 1	block H1274
6d	early morning return	booking numbers	block H1479
1/2	early morning return	booking number 1	block H0717

The 4d EMR is unusual, the 1952 fare scale not providing for such a fare. As has been explained in the section on fares, this was for a sub-standard fare between Corporation Bridge and Cleveland Bridge.

 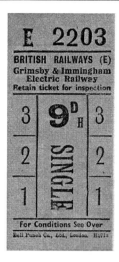   

Early 1953
Printer: Bell Punch Co
Title: BRITISH RAILWAYS (E)

left: back - Singles, block A3863

right: back - EMRs, block A3862

16th August 1953

Early morning fares (only) were increased and tickets by Bell Punch exactly as those above were produced to cover the four new fares. No fare scale letter was shown on these tickets, which were:-

10d	early morning return	booking numbers 1-4	block H2644
1/-	early morning return	booking numbers 1-3	block H2642
1/2	early morning return	booking numbers 1-2	block H2643
1/4	early morning return	booking number 1	block H2645

16th August 1953
Printer: Bell Punch Co
Title: BRITISH RAILWAYS (E)

Late 1953

Further reprints by Bell Punch as those above, except that the 6d early morning return used the single back (block A3863) instead of the correct early morning return back. The singles still show the fare scale letter "H" (correctly, since the 1952 fares still applied for singles), the 6d early morning return shows no fare scale letter and the 1/4 early morning return shows fare scale letter "J" (probably in error, since no other Grimsby and Immingham ticket is known with this fare scale letter). Tickets known are:-

2d	single	booking numbers 1-5	block H3160
4d	single	booking numbers 1-4	block H3164
5½d	child single	booking numbers 1-2	block H3161
6d	early morning return	booking numbers 1-5	block H3162
1/4	early morning return	booking number 1	block H2673

Late 1953:
Printer: Bell Punch Co
Title: BRITISH RAILWAYS (E)

1954

Reprint by Bell Punch as those above, except that the heading is now British Transport Commission on both front and back and the conditions are modified (without otherwise changing the wording) to refer to that body instead of the Railway Executive. The new back, with the correct early morning return validity, is on block A4908. Only one ticket is known:-

8d   early morning return   booking numbers 1-5   block H4764

1954
Printer: Bell Punch Co.
Title: BRITISH TRANSPORT COMMISSION (E)
back: block A4908

5th June 1955

All fares (both single and early morning return) increased and tickets by Bell Punch produced to cover the new fares. These had British Transport Commission heading on the front as for the last item, but new back blocks were produced - A5363 for singles and A5364 for early morning returns. The backs now had the correct wording of the BTC conditions rather than a modified version of the Railway Executive conditions. None of these tickets had a fare scale letter. The block numbers shown on the tickets are a mixture of H35xx and H65xx numbers - it seems probable that the former are errors for the corresponding H65xx numbers. Tickets known are:-

8d	single	booking numbers 1-4	block H3519
10d	single	booking numbers 1-3	block H3524
1/-	single	booking numbers 1-2	block H6516
1/2	single	booking number 1	block H6525
6d	child single	booking numbers 1-2	block H6520
7d	child single	booking number 1	block H6522
9d	early morning return	booking numbers 1-5	block H6513
1/-	early morning return	booking numbers 1-4	block H6517
1/2	early morning return	booking numbers 1-3	block H6514
1/4	early morning return	booking numbers 1-2	block H6518
1/6	early morning return	booking number 1	block H6521

4d and 5d child singles should also exist, but have not been seen

above: back - Singles, block A5363
below: back - EMRs, block A5364

5 June 1955
Printer: Bell Punch Co.
Title: BRITISH TRANSPORT COMMISSION (E)

1st July 1956

The line was cut back to Cleveland Bridge and new tickets with reduced numbers of bookings were produced. There seem to have been two printings of these - a few tickets with H82xx block numbers, followed by a near complete set with H84xx block numbers. There was also evidently confusion as to exactly how many bookings needed to be included on the 6d EMR, as versions exist showing different numbers. The fronts of these tickets were exactly as previous issues, but further different printings of the backs were used - block A5545 on singles and A5922 on early morning returns for most issues, but a few tickets had the old early morning return back on block A5364 or a slightly different single back on block A5365. Tickets known are:-

(a) with back blocks A5364/5

1/-	single	booking number	1	block H8252
1/-	single	booking number	1	block H8424
6d	early morning return	booking numbers	1-5	block H8258
1/-	early morning return	booking numbers	1-3	block H8254
1/4	early morning return	booking number	1	block H8255

(b) with back blocks A5545/5922

2d	single	booking numbers	1-3	block H8429
4d	single	booking numbers	1-6	block H8412
6d	single	booking numbers	1-6	block H8414
8d	single	booking numbers	1-3	block H8524
10d	single	booking numbers	1-2	block H8422
1/-	single	booking number	1	block H8424
1d	child single	booking numbers	1-3	block H8428
2d	child single	booking numbers	1-6	block H8413
3d	child single	booking numbers	1-6	block H8415
4d	child single	booking numbers	1-3	block H8523
5d	child single	booking numbers	1-2	block H8423
6d	child single	booking number	1	block H8425
6d	early morning return	booking numbers	1-6	block H8409
9d	early morning return	booking numbers	1-3	block H8430
1/2	early morning return	booking numbers	1-2	block H8405

1 July 1956
Printer: Bell Punch Co.
Title: BRITISH TRANSPORT
COMMISSION (E)

back - Singles, block A5545, some
Singles had block A5365

back - EMRs, block A5922, some EMRs
had old block A5364

15th September 1957

Early morning fares (only) were increased and tickets exactly as those above, with back block A5922, were produced to cover the five new fares. These tickets were:-

7d	early morning return	booking numbers 1-5	block J0947
10d	early morning return	booking numbers 1-3	block J0948
1/1	early morning return	booking numbers 1-3	block J0949
1/4	early morning return	booking numbers 1-2	block J0950
1/6	early morning return	booking number 1	block J0951

15 September 1957
Printer: Bell Punch Co.
Title: BRITISH TRANSPORT COMMISSION (E)

back - block A5922

28th September 1959

The fare structure was completely changed following the withdrawal of the off-peak service and a new set of single, child single, special cheap day and child special cheap day tickets by Williamson were produced. These were similar in design to the earlier Bell Punch issues, but the singles were a brighter shade of green and the child overprints were distinctly different. They had Williamson's imprint and customer reference number B5 at the bottom. No validity was shown on the backs of the singles, just conditions, but the special cheap days showed "Valid Day of Issue". There was evidently more than one printing of some values, since tickets are known with distinctly different value figures. The tickets known are:-

3d	single	booking numbers 1-3
5d	single	booking numbers 1-4
8d	single	booking numbers 1-4
10d	single	booking numbers 1-2
11d	single	booking number 1
1/1	single	booking numbers 1-2
1/3	single	booking number 1
1½d	child single	booking numbers 1-3
2½d	child single	booking numbers 1-4
1/2	special cheap day	booking numbers 1-4
1/6	special cheap day	booking numbers 1-2
1/8	special cheap day	booking number 1
1/10	special cheap day	booking number 1
2/1	special cheap day	booking numbers 1-2
7d	child special cheap day	booking numbers 1-4
9d	child special cheap day	booking numbers 1-2
10d	child special cheap day	booking number 1
11d	child special cheap day	booking number 1
1/0½d	child special cheap day	booking numbers 1-2

There were also two exchange tickets, for Grimsby Cleveland Bdge and Kiln Lane Stallingborough/ Immingham Town or Dock, dark blue with the "Valid Day of Issue" back, for issue in exchange for return halves of bus tickets.

Singles

Special Cheap Days

Exchange Tickets

British Transport Commission (E)

Issued subject to the Regulations and Conditions in the Commission's publications and Notices applicable to British Railways.

NOT TRANSFERABLE

back- Singles

British Transport Commission (E)

VALID DAY OF ISSUE

Issued subject to the Regulations and Conditions in the Commission's Publications and Notices applicable to British Railways.

NOT TRANSFERABLE

back - Special Cheap Days and Exchange Tickets

28 September 1959
Printer: Williamson
Title: BRITISH TRANSPORT COMMISSION (E)

BRITISH RAILWAYS

GRIMSBY AND IMMINGHAM ELECTRIC RAILWAY

CARS LEAVE
WEEKDAYS

GRIMSBY (Corporation Bridge)

a.m.	a.m.	p.m.	p.m.
12 50	9 50	4 50	4 50
1 50	10 20	4 50	5 0SX
3 0	10 50	5 20	5 5SX
4 15	11 20	5 50	5 20
5 20	11 50	6 20	5 50
5 50		6 50	6 20
6 20	p.m.	7 20	6 50
6 50	12 20	7 50	7 20
7 10	12 50	8 50	7 50
7 20	1 20	9 20	8 20
7 50	1 50	9 50	9 20
8 20	2 20	10 50	9 50
8 20	2 50	10 50	10 20
8 50	3 20	11 20	10 50
9 20	3 50		11 20SX

SO—Saturdays only   SX—Saturdays excepted

IMMINGHAM DOCK

a.m.	a.m.	p.m.	p.m.
12 20	10 50		4 50
1 20	11 20		5 0SX
2 20	11 50		5 5SX
3 45	noon		5 20
4 45	12 0SO		5 50
5 50			6 20
6 20	p.m.		6 50
6 50	12 20		7 20
7 20	12 50		7 50
7 50	1 20		8 20
8 20	1 50		9 20
8 50	2 20		9 50
9 20	2 50		10 20
9 50	3 20		10 50
10 20	3 50		11 20SX
	4 20		

SUNDAYS

GRIMSBY (Corporation Bridge)

a.m.	a.m.	p.m.	p.m.
12 50	10 20	5 20	5 5
1 50	11 20	5 50	5 20
3 0	p.m.	6 20	5 50
4 35A	12 20	7 20	6 50
5 20	1 20	8 20	7 50
7 0	2 20	9 20	8 50
7 20	3 20	10 20	9 50
8 40	4 20	11 20	10 20
9 20	4 35		10 50

IMMINGHAM DOCK

a.m.	a.m.	p.m.	p.m.
12 20	11 50	5 5	5 5
1 20	p.m.	5 20	5 20
2 30	12 50	6 50	5 50
3 45	1 50	8 50	6 50
4 58A	2 50	9 50	7 50
6 0	3 50	10 20	8 50
7 20	4 5	10 50	9 50
8 40	4 20		10 20
10 50	4 50		10 50

A—To and from Immingham Town only

The cars stop at
YARBORO' STREET   CLEVELAND BRIDGE
STORTFORD STREET   IMMINGHAM TOWN
and by request at
JACKSON STREET   GREAT COATES LEVEL CROSSING
BOULEVARD RECREATION GROUND   No. 5 PASSING PLACE
CLEVELAND STREET   MARSH ROAD LEVEL CROSSING
KILN LANE, STALLINGBOROUGH
THIS SERVICE IS SUBJECT TO REVISION. PARTICULARS OF ANY
ALTERATIONS MADE WILL BE ANNOUNCED

London, September 1952.

Published by The Railway Executive (Eastern Region) PP.143/16. Printed in Great Britain. W. A. SMITH (Leeds) LTD. C.4
B.R. 35001

REVISED PASSENGER FARES
FROM 1st SEPTEMBER 1952

	Ordinary single s. d.	Early morning return s. d.
GRIMSBY (Corporation Bridge) and		
Beeson Street	2	—
Cleveland Street	2	—
Cleveland Bridge	4	4
Great Coates Level Crossing	4	6
No. 5 Passing Place	6	8
Marsh Road Level Crossing	9	11
Kiln Lane, Stallingborough	9	11
Immingham Town	11	1 0
Immingham Dock	1 1	1 2
BEESON STREET and		
Cleveland Street	2	—
Cleveland Bridge	2	—
Great Coates Level Crossing	4	6
No. 5 Passing Place	6	8
Marsh Road Level Crossing	7	9
Kiln Lane, Stallingborough	9	11
Immingham Town	9	11
Immingham Dock	1 1	1 2
CLEVELAND STREET and		
Cleveland Bridge	2	—
Great Coates Level Crossing	4	6
No. 5 Passing Place	6	8
Marsh Road Level Crossing	7	9
Kiln Lane, Stallingborough	9	11
Immingham Town	9	11
Immingham Dock	11	1 0

	Ordinary single s. d.	Early morning return s. d.
CLEVELAND BRIDGE and		
Great Coates Level Crossing	2	—
No. 5 Passing Place	4	6
Marsh Road Level Crossing	6	8
Kiln Lane, Stallingborough	7	9
Immingham Town	9	11
Immingham Dock	11	1 0
GREAT COATES LEVEL CROSSING and		
No. 5 Passing Place	4	6
Marsh Road Level Crossing	6	8
Kiln Lane, Stallingborough	6	8
Immingham Town	7	9
Immingham Dock	9	11
No. 5 PASSING PLACE and		
Marsh Road Level Crossing	4	6
Kiln Lane, Stallingborough	4	6
Immingham Town	6	8
Immingham Dock	7	9
MARSH ROAD LEVEL CROSSING and		
Kiln Lane, Stallingborough	2	—
Immingham Town	4	6
Immingham Dock	6	8
KILN LANE, STALLINGBOROUGH and		
Immingham Town	2	—
Immingham Dock	4	8
IMMINGHAM TOWN and		
Immingham Dock	4	6

AVAILABILITY

Ordinary tickets
Single tickets — 3 days
Return tickets at double single fare 3 months

Children under three years of age are conveyed free, and those of three and under fourteen at half-fare with a minimum of one penny for each journey.

Early Morning Return tickets
Outward—By any car arriving destination at or before 8.0 a.m.
Return—By any car on day of issue only
Children are charged the Adult Early Morning Return fare

Weekly Season ticket
Grimsby (Corporation Bridge) and Cleveland Bridge 4/-

Season tickets
Particulars of rates and conditions obtainable at Grimsby and Immingham or from the DISTRICT COMMERCIAL SUPERINTENDENT, LINCOLN

Tickets are issued subject to the Executive's Bye-Laws, Regulations and Conditions

Copies of the Bye-Laws and Regulations will be found exhibited at stations

A booklet showing the conditions upon which tickets, including season tickets are issued and the regulations and conditions applicable to passengers' luggage, can be obtained free of charge from the station booking office.

British Railways timetable - 1st September 1952

426—2 OPENING AND CLOSING OF STATIONS★
Grimsby and Immingham Electric Railway

On and from 1st July, 1956, the section of the Grimsby and Immingham Electric Railway, approximately one mile and a quarter in length, between Grimsby Corporation Bridge and Cleveland Bridge will be abandoned, and the present electric tram service between Grimsby Corporation Bridge and Immingham Dock will then be operated only between Grimsby Cleveland Bridge and Immingham Dock.

Concurrently with the termination of the tramway service within the Borough of Grimsby, the Corporation Transport Department will institute new 'bus services between various parts of the Borough and the Tramway Terminus at Cleveland Bridge to connect with the trams which will continue to run between that point and Immingham Dock broadly on the basis of the existing service. The new omnibus service will traverse the route now taken by the tramcars between Corporation Bridge and Cleveland Bridge and there will be no actual loss of transport facilities.

Existing fares applicable with Immingham Dock and Killingholme via Grimsby and Electric Cars are cancelled on and from 1st July, 1956, and stations recording fares must withdraw the forms from their records and send immediately to my Fares Office, Fenchurch Street referring to F/1/Pad 118. Through bookings, which will not include conveyance by Grimsby Corporation 'bus services to and from Cleveland Bridge, may continue to be given, but application for new fares should only be made as and when the demand arises.

F/6/Pad 22—495

2

*Extract from British Railways Traffic Circular announcing
the cutback of the line to Cleveland Bridge - 1st July 1956*

Bookings other than singles and early morning returns were much less affected by the 1952 Charges Scheme, and there was no reason for a complete reprint of the tickets. The only new facility was the ordinary return (which replaced the previous monthly return) and even for these bookings it was common practice for monthly return tickets to be used up as ordinary returns. It is clear that this is what was done on the Grimsby and Immingham and other pre-1952 tickets certainly were used up also. Apart from two sets of Harland printed tickets, the earliest evidence of large scale reprinting is a batch of tickets of various types on Bell Punch blocks in the H12xx series, dating from about early 1953.

The tickets we are concerned with in this section went through the same sequence as the singles and early morning returns, with a few Harland prints, Bell Punch prints with British Railways and later British Transport Commission

headings and finally some Williamson prints. Backs were generally as on the early morning returns (i.e. "Valid as Dated by Authorised Trams", but some later Bell Punch prints had "...Authorised Trains" in error and a few tickets had specialised backs. Colours were generally as for the earlier Edmondson printed tickets, although it should be noted that the width of the Bell Punch and Williamson stripes is about 1½ - 2mm

A number of tickets are known only as printers proofs without serial numbers. Some of these were clearly never issued in the form indicated (e.g. the Cleveland Bridge tickets with BR(E) heading and the tickets with LNER style backs), but others may well have been. These printers proofs have thus all been included in the list that follows, but are indicated with an asterisk. Tickets recorded are:-

Return Corporation Bridge and Immingham Dock - white, wide green bar at left hand side.

2/2	Bell Punch block H1278 BR(E) heading	back block A3862
2/2H	Bell Punch block H3242 BR(E) heading	back block A3862

Child return Corporation Bridge and Immingham Dock
- white, wide green bar at left hand side and vertical red skeleton child overprint.

1/1	Bell Punch block H1277 BR(E) heading	back block A3862

back:
block A3862

Service Military etc. single Cleveland Bridge to Immingham Dock - green.

* -	Bell Punch block H8410 BR(E) heading	back blank
* -	Bell Punch block H8410 BTC(E) heading	back block A5547

Service Military etc. return Cleveland Bridge to Immingham Dock - green.

* -	Bell Punch block H8427 BTC(E) heading	back block A6002

Forces leave single Corporation Bridge to Immingham Dock - white, wide pink bar at left hand side.

10dH	Harland BR(E) heading	"3 months" back

Forces leave single Cleveland Bridge to Immingham Dock - white, wide pink bar at left hand side.

9d	Bell Punch block H8408 BTC(E) heading	back block A5545

Forces leave return Corporation Bridge to Immingham Dock - white, wide pink bar at left hand side.

1/8H	Harland BR(E) heading	"3 months" back
1/8H	Bell Punch block H1474 BR(E) heading	back block A4018

Forces leave return Cleveland Bridge to Immingham Dock - white, wide pink bar at left hand side.

* 1/6	Bell Punch block H8406 BTC(E) heading	back block A5841

Service Military etc:

back: blank

back: block A5547

back: block A6002

back:
block A5547

back:
block A6002

Forces Leave Single

back: block
A5545

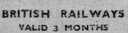

Forces Leave Return

Harland
print

Forces Leave Return

back: block
A5841

back:
block A4018?

Free pass Cleveland Bridge and Immingham Dock - white
* * -   Bell Punch block H9870 LNER heading   back block A6208
*   -   Bell Punch block H9870 no heading   back block A6208

BRITISH TRANSPORT COMMISSION
1. This Free Ticket is NOT transferable and is available between the places named for one journey.
2. It is issued subject to the Regulations and Conditions in the Commissions Publications and Notices applicable to British Railways. A6208

both backs:
block A6208

Privilege return Corporation Bridge and Immingham Town - blue, two vertical red stripes.
    7½d   Bell Punch block H1278 BR(E) heading   back block A3862

Privilege return Cleveland Bridge and Immingham Town - blue, two vertical red stripes.
    6d   Bell Punch block H8711 BTC(E) heading   back block A5011
    6d   Bell Punch block J0508 BTC(E) heading   back block A5011

Child privilege return Cleveland Bridge and Immingham Town
              - blue, two vertical red stripes and vertical red skeleton child overprint.
    3d   Williamson   BTC(E) heading   "Auth Trams" back

Privilege return Corporation Bridge and Immingham Dock - magenta, two vertical blue stripes.
  * 8½d   Bell Punch block H1279 BR(E) heading   back block A3963
    8½d   Bell Punch block H1279 BR(E) heading   back block A3862

Privilege return Cleveland Bridge and Immingham Dock - magenta, two vertical blue stripes.
    7½d   Bell Punch block H8708 BTC(E) heading   back block A5011
    7½d   Bell Punch block J0509 BTC(E) heading   back block A5011

Child privilege return Corporation Bridge and Immingham Dock
              - magenta, two vertical blue stripes and vertical red skeleton child overprint.
  * 4½d   Bell Punch block H1276 BR(E) heading   back block A3963

Child privilege return Cleveland Bridge and Immingham Dock
              - magenta, two vertical blue stripes and vertical red skeleton child overprint.
    4d   Bell Punch block H8709 BTC(E) heading   back block A5011
    4d   Bell Punch block J0510 BTC(E) heading   back block A5011

back:
block A3862
see Return

BRITISH TRANSPORT COMMISSION (E)
VALID AS DATED BY AUTHORISED TRAINS
Issued subject to the Regulations and Conditions in the Commission's Publications and Notices applicable to British Railways. A5011
NOT TRANSFERABLE

back: block
A5011

This Series of Tickets is for issue only to Company's Servants, their Wives or Children in accordance with the Special Regulations as to Privilege Tickets.

Any other person using this Ticket will be prosecuted.   A3963

NOT TRANSFERABLE.

back:
block A3963

back: block A3862
see previous page

British Transport Commission (E)

VALID AS DATED BY
AUTHORISED TRAMS

Issued subject to the Regulations and Conditions in the Commission's publications and Notices applicable to British Railways.

NOT TRANSFERABLE

Williamson print

back: block A3963
see above

back: block A5011
see previous page

Dog single Corporation Bridge to Immingham Town - magenta
* **8d**   Bell Punch block H1280 BR(E) heading   back block A3966

Dog single Cleveland Bridge to Immingham Dock - magenta
* **9d**   Bell Punch block H8432 BTC(E) heading   back block A5922
  5d   Bell Punch block H9416 BTC(E) heading   back block A6061
  5d   Williamson   BTC(E) heading   "No Validity" back

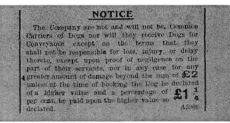

reverse:
block A3966

reverse:
block A5922

back: block
A6061

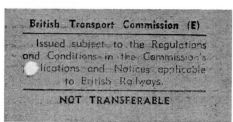

Williamson
print

Dog return Cleveland Bridge to Immingham Dock - magenta
* **8d**   Bell Punch block H9414   BTC(E) heading   back block A5715
  8d   Bell Punch block H9414   BTC(E) heading   back block A6061
  8d   Williamson   BTC(E) heading   "No Validity" back

back:
block A5715

back: block A6061
see Dog Single

back -see Williamson
Dog Single

Bicycle or Perambulator single Corporation Bridge and Immingham Dock - yellow.
* **1/2**   Bell Punch block H1275 BR(E) heading   back block A1964

Bicycle or Perambulator single Cleveland Bridge and Immingham Dock - yellow.
* **1/3**   Bell Punch block H8433 BR(E) heading   back block A5922
  1/3   Bell Punch block H8431 BTC(E) heading   back block A5922

back:
block A1964

back of both: block A5922
- see Dog Single

Privilege Bicycle or Perambulator single Corporation Bridge and Immingham Dock
- yellow with two vertical red stripes.

    1/-   Bell Punch block H6680 BTC(E) heading   back block A5406

Privilege Bicycle or Perambulator single Cleveland Bridge and Immingham Dock
- yellow with two vertical red stripes.

    1/-   Bell Punch block H8431 BTC(E) heading   back block A5936

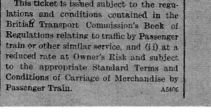

back:
block A5406

back:
block A5936

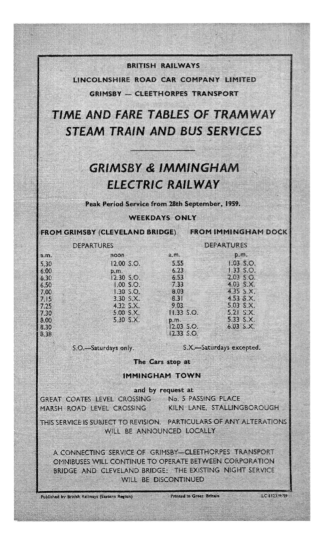

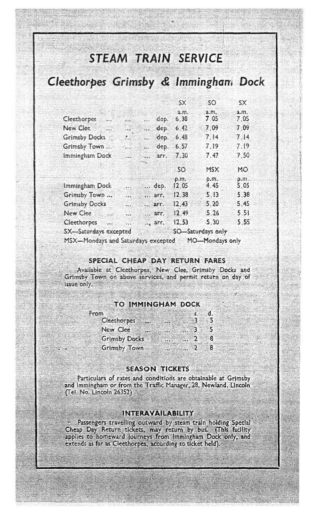

British Railways timetable from the start of the peak-period only service - 28th September 1959

10 - Other Miscellaneous Tickets - Post-1952

The existence of season tickets covering the Grimsby & Immingham has been noted in the chapter on fares, and a 1954 BR(E) example issued at Grimsby (Corporation Bridge) has been seen. It seems likely that any other issues would have been of standard GCR, LNER or BR design and they would presumably have been issued through the office at Corporation Bridge (later Cleveland Bridge) and perhaps at Immingham Dock railway station (the terminus of the branch from Goxhill). Six and seven day weekly workmans tickets in Edmondson card format have been seen, and are detailed in the chapter on LNER workmans tickets. These were probably also issued at the office at Corporation Bridge.

Interavailability of return tickets between tram, bus and train after 1959 has already been mentioned. The arrangements, applying between Grimsby and Immingham Dock/Kiln Lane only, were:-

Outward Journey	Return Journey	Ticketing
Tram	Bus	Exchange ticket probably issued on bus. (Facility only available outside hours of tramway operation.)
Tram	Train	Excess fare paid at destination (see below). (These arrangements applied also to *outward* halves of tram special cheap day tickets, presumably those issued in advance as prepaids.)
Bus	Tram	Exchange ticket (see page 42) issued on tram.
Bus	Train	Tickets not valid.
Train	Tram	Train ticket accepted and clipped on tram.
Train	Bus	Exchange ticket probably issued on bus.

Any exchange ticket issued on the bus is likely to have been a normal machine issue of the operator concerned, and excess paid on tram tickets used by train could have been dealt with by a normal blank paper excess receipt. However, preprinted paper excess receipts are known for the difference between the tram fare and the EMR by the workman's train. (This facility must have predated the cutback in the tram service since a printer's proof of one such ticket is known with a November 1956 date. This may well have been new stock being produced following the closure of the street tramway section earlier that year.). Other special tickets arising out of these arrangements were the punch type exchange tickets issued on the tram and the early morning returns for the train service. The former have been described in the section on post 1952 tickets; the latter were standard BTC Edmondson card EMRs routed "via Humber Road Junction" and with a letter "B" in the text of the return half to indicate return availability by tram or bus.

The arrangement described above was not the only example of interavailability involving the tramway. Workman's returns (and later EMRs) from Grimsby Town and stations beyond to Great Coates (on the main line west of Grimsby and about half a mile from Great Coates Level Crossing) were also available between Corporation Bridge and Great Coates Level Crossing. This interavailability was shown on both halves of the tickets concerned. The arrangement existed by 1942 and a ticket showing it dated 10th October 1956 is known, although nothing has been seen showing alternative availability between *Cleveland* Bridge and Great Coates.

Weekly Season Ticket

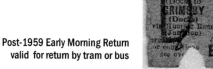

Post-1959 Early Morning Return valid for return by tram or bus

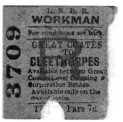

Workman's Returns and EMR to Great Coates showing alternate availability on the Grimsby & Immingham

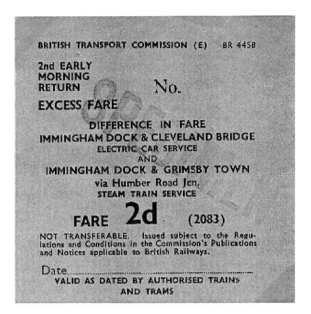

Paper pad Excess Tickets issued to holders of tramway tickets when returning by train.

Through bookings from railway stations to Immingham Dock via Grimsby and the tramway are known to have existed from LNER days. In most cases blank card tickets would probably have been used - one such from Gainsborough Central on a Period Reduced Fare blank, perhaps for the "Merchantile Marine Leave" facility, is known. However, as late as 1956 Kings Cross was issuing standard BTC style printed third class singles to "Immingham Dock via Peakirk, Grimsby & Electric Cars". There were also fares via Grimsby (Town/Corporation Bridge) and Immingham (tram terminus/station) to Killingholme, but no ticket for this booking has been seen. Use was probably minimal, the all-rail route via Goxhill being preferable to crossing both Grimsby (from Town station to Corporation Bridge) and Immingham (from tram terminus to the station at Western Jetty).

Finally, mention must be made of tickets issued by the Light Railway Transport League for trips organised by them by special car on the tramway. These were thin cards 1½" x 3½", in a design used by LRTL for special trips on a number of different tramway systems, the following having been seen from the Grimsby & Immingham:-

15th August 1948	5/-	orange
4th June 1950	2/-	pink
10th June 1956	3/-	grey
21st June 1956	3/6	blue on white

To these must be added the special tickets said to have been issued at the Corporation Bridge office at a fare of 4d for travel by the last car from Corporation Bridge to Cleveland Bridge on the night of 30th June 1956, returning by bus. Unfortunately this choice ticket has not been seen.

Light Railway Transport League -
Special Tour ticket - 15th August 1948

Car 31 at Cleveland Road, 10 June 1956

[J C Gillham]

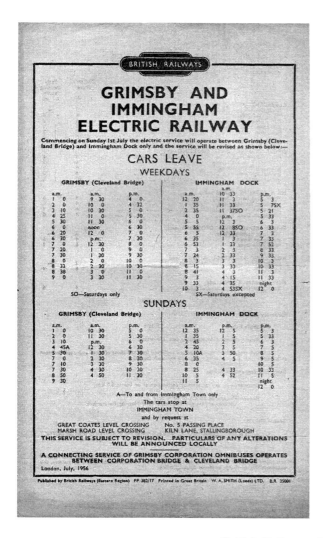

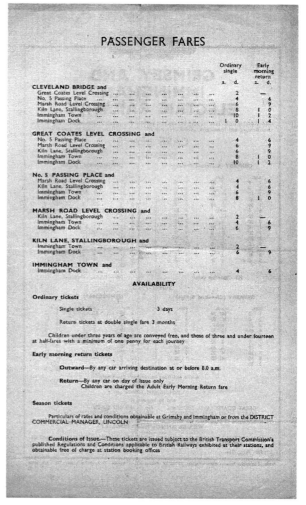

British Railways timetable - July 1956

Appendix - Basis of Railway Fares

In order to understand the fares background to the tickets of the Grimsby & Immingham Tramway, it is necessary to know, in outline, the basic principles which applied to railway fares over the years. Prior to the First World War there was no standard rate for railway fares, although 1d per mile was a common basis for ordinary third class singles. Other types of fare were far more arbitrary. This applied particularly to workman's fares, which were often very low (a nominal 1d per journey - i.e. 2d return - was a common rate, particularly in urban areas).

When revisions were made during and after the war, these took the form of standard percentage increases applied to the fare applicable immediately prior to the first (1917) revision. These increases were 50% (from 1st January 1917), 75% (from 6th August 1920; 1st September for workmen's fares) and a reduction to 50% (from 1st January 1923). The 1917 increase was designed to discourage non-essential travel, rather than raise extra revenue, and did not apply to either workman's fares or season ticket rates. The 1920 increase did apply to these however, and so far as workman's fares were concerned there was a new mileage scale giving fares slightly below the general level of the 1920 single fares (assuming a 1d per mile base up to 1917). There was also a provision limiting the permitted increase on existing workman's fares. One source says that the limit was an increase of 200%, another that the increase should not exceed 4d on a daily ticket - both are a reflection of the very low levels of fare which had applied on some lines.

Following the grouping, an attempt was made to produce a national standard for railway fares, which was introduced from 1st January 1928. This provided for third class single fares at 1½d per mile and first class singles at 2½d per mile with other fares related to this. Despite the existence of a standard, however, many non-standard (particularly below standard) fares still survived. The scheme provided that these below standard fares should not be increased by more than 10% (for ordinary fares) and 1d per day or 6d per week (for workman's fares). (Despite all this however, there was nothing to stop new sub-standard fares being introduced subsequently to meet specific competitive circumstances, and this was indeed done when needed.)

Subsequent revisions were again on the basis of overall percentage increases, in this case to the 1928 fare. In practice revisions were carried out by issuing conversion scales showing the 'base' (1928) fare, the fare immediately prior to the increase, and the new fare. There are two important points to note about the system - (1) the 1928 fare (whether standard or not) remained the base throughout, and (2) the scale applied equally to any fare whether standard or not. Thus, for example, a 2½d fare became, say, 3½d regardless of whether it was the correct fare at 1½d per mile or not. Also, as a result, if the 1928 fare for a particular journey was substandard it generally remained so through all subsequent revisions. Under this system revisions were made as follows:-

		Increase over 1928 base		
		Ordinary	Workman's	Seasons
1st Oct 1937	"N" fares	+ 5%	no change	+ 5%
1st May 1940	"R" fares	+ 15½%	+ 10%	+ 15½%
1st Dec 1940	"C" fares	+ 22½%	+ 10%	+ 15½%
1st Jul 1946	"P" fares	+ 40%	+ 25%	+ 31½%
1st Oct 1947	"Z" fares	+ 62¾%	+ 55%	+ 62¾%

The code letters shown were used to refer to the various levels of fare, and in some cases (although not normally on the Grimsby and Immingham) appeared on tickets. These increases applied to all fares, including monthly returns, a single fare and a third return ticket introduced in the mid-1930s which gradually replaced the ordinary return. However, monthly returns also had an additional increase of 10%, the "E" fares from 1st January 1952. There were also additional increases affecting only accompanied traffic, to give the "A" scale of 15th May 1950 and the "B" scale of 9th April 1951.

Following nationalisation, 1952 saw a further major change in the basis of railway fares with the introduction (partially from 1st May and in full from 1st September) of the B.T.C. Passenger Charges Scheme. In this scheme all fares were recalculated strictly on mileage with third class single fares at 1¾d per mile, ordinary returns (replacing monthly returns) at twice single fare, and early morning returns (replacing workman's returns) on a tapering mileage scale.

The only exceptions were fares which were so substandard that raising them to the correct level would have resulted in increases of more than 20%. In these cases it was laid down that the fares should be increased by 20% at the introduction of the scheme and at each subsequent revision, thus eventually bringing them up to standard.

The first stage of the scheme (1st May 1952) was the introduction of those fares which were either unchanged or reduced, and the second stage (1st September 1952) those fares which were increased. Code letter "H" was used to indicate the new 1952 fares. Subsequent revisions were again made by scale to scale increases starting from the 1952 base. Such increases were made from 16th August 1953 (early morning returns only - code "J"), 5th June 1955 and 15th September 1957 (early morning returns only). The next general increase, from 2nd November 1959, did not affect the Grimsby & Immingham since by this time a completely non-standard fare structure had been introduced.

Other Publications